Old Virginia Houses

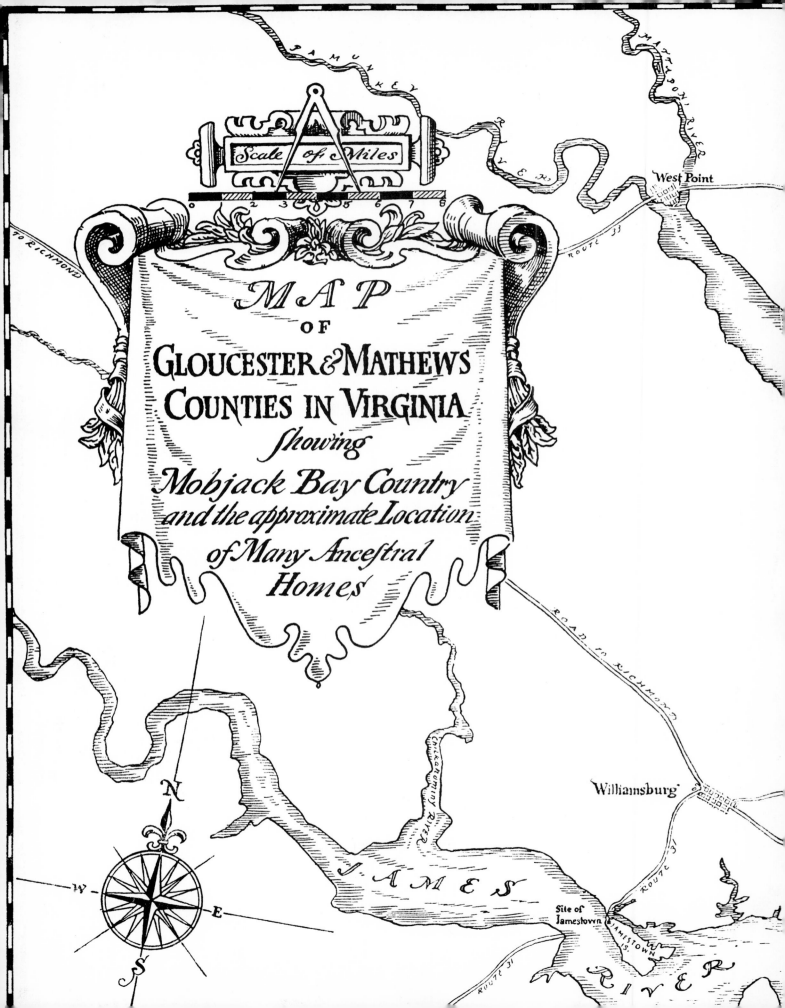

Old Virginia Houses

THE MOBJACK BAY COUNTRY

BY

EMMIE FERGUSON FARRAR

ILLUSTRATED WITH PHOTOGRAPHS BY

HARRY BAGBY & OTHERS

BONANZA BOOKS • NEW YORK

F
227
F3
v.1

THIS SERIES AS A WHOLE IS FOR

FRANKLIN FLOYD FARRAR

THIS VOLUME IS FOR

Nina Taliaferro Sanders

CONTENTS

ILLUSTRATIONS

FOREWORD

WITH the reawakening throughout the country in Colonial Architecture, thousands of tourists each year make pilgrimages to the old homes of Virginia. Nowhere in America is there to be seen a greater exhibition of Colonial Architecture, of English origin, than in Tidewater Virginia.

Tidewater Virginia is just what the term implies. It is all that territory of Virginia contiguous to the Chesapeake Bay and its estuaries. In it the English made their first permanent settlement in America. Here, from the crudest pioneer conditions flowered a civilization that assembled the first representative legislative body on the American Continent. It was in that cradle of democracy that trial by jury was first instituted, on the narrow peninsula between the James and York Rivers.

British dominion in the United States had its beginning at Jamestown only twelve miles from where it ended at Yorktown. Physically this region is little changed since the "Golden Age," or half-century preceding the American Revolution. It has continued consistently pastoral, a haven from hurry and standardization of twentieth century life. There is still Arcadian simplicity in this land of water.

The old houses dealt with in this book are located in Gloucester and Mathews Counties, in the heart of Tidewater Virginia. These counties are not matched elsewhere in number and variety of old houses in various stages of survival or restoration.

The very isolation of this region where communication was once almost solely by water has spared many of its fine old houses the destruction that progress would have brought them.

Among the glories of Gloucester and Mathews today, are numerous surviving mansions that were owned and occupied by celebrated personages, or were the scenes of historic events which greatly influenced our national character and institutions.

This region affords the student of Colonial Architecture a great opportunity to study the development of the early house, from the medieval cottage of one room and loft, to the great Georgian mansion, symbol of eighteenth-century living.

Time and again attempts have been made to simplify the subject of old houses for the benefit of the layman, with disastrous results. Where romance and tradition are concerned many people respond to their emotions rather than their intellect.

The pioneer student of Colonial Architecture, of a generation ago, assumed that when the seventeenth century was over, the colonists graduated suddenly from the straw thatched huts of Jamestown and Henrico City to the great plantation manors of Westover and Rosewell. These great houses were developed, not invented.

Only in the last quarter of a century has any patient or prolonged study been given to the transitional examples that form a missing link between the medieval and classical styles.

It might be said that the medieval period in Virginia architecture began with the landing of the first settlers at Jamestown in 1607, and ended with the building of the Governor's Palace at Williamsburg in 1706. The building of the Governor's Palace in 1706 marked the beginning of Georgian Architecture in Virginia, which is divided into three periods: Early Georgian 1706 to 1750, Mid-Georgian 1750 to 1765, Late Georgian 1765 to 1776.

It is true that most of the houses built during the Seventeenth Century have disappeared, taken in the toll of time, fire and the elements. Nevertheless, traces and documents and credible tradition make possible a good general idea of the evolution of the early house.

Under the Civil Works Administration in 1933, a great number of unemployed architects and draftsmen supplied a highly trained personnel, fitted by antiquarian interest and architectural experience to make a survey of Historic American Buildings.

When several hundred photographs and floor plans of many kinds of structures were gathered together over a period of years, we came unexpectedly and very much by accident upon the subject of the transition which comprises a new chapter in the history of American Architecture.

The transition is a development in architecture which may be summed up as follows: A step toward the Georgian goal of more space, more balance and more formality; a period of experimental stepping stones toward more elegance and gracious living which marked the eighteenth century.

FOREWORD

In attempting to establish the age of any old house, one has to discover what changes have been made in the course of the years in its structure, and when. This is often difficult to do, in many instances almost impossible, and therefore we have to rely on analogy and deduction. All houses cannot be dated from the fact that they have the same features as houses of known dates, even in the same general locality, as there were "carry overs" (so to speak) where styles persisted long after they were supposed to have ended.

The author has made no attempt to establish the date of origin on the old houses in this book by their structural features, but only through surviving documents and credible tradition. It is well written in simple everyday language from the viewpoint of the layman, and contains much information not available elsewhere. It is copiously illustrated with rare photographs whose subjects in many instances disappeared more than a half-century ago.

JOHN FRANCIS SPEIGHT

APPRECIATION

IN the preparation of the manuscript for this book, I wish to express appreciation, first of all to Nina Taliaferro Sanders, (Mrs. H. O. Sanders), who knows and loves the "Mobjack Bay Country" as no one else does, and who gives so freely, with love and enthusiasm:

To the late Dr. Douglas Southall Freeman, who encouraged me in my work for almost a quarter of a century.

To Dr. Gertrude R. B. Richards, who is experienced in research, possibly more thoroughly, than any scholar now living, and who has given of that knowledge so freely;

To Mr. and Mrs. Webster S. Rhoads, Jr., of Elmington, for lending unpublished manuscripts and pictures, and for bringing me in contact with Mrs. Sanders;

To Mr. and Mrs. William Ingles, of White Marsh, who gave much information;

To Dr. and Mrs. H. Page Mauck, of Richmond and Gloucester, who so kindly checked much data, and gave much information;

To Miss Dahlia Callis, of the Mathews Public Library, who gave much information;

To Mr. and Mrs. Wesley C. Morck, of Belleville;

To Mr. and Mrs. Theodore Pratt, of Little England;

To Mr. and Mrs. Gordon Bolitho, of Toddsbury;

To Major and Mrs. Jeffrey Montague, of Lowland Cottage;

To Mr. and Mrs. F. Higginson Cabot, of Green Plains;

To Mr. and Mrs. A. P. Blood, of Auburn;

To Mr. and Mrs. Hope Norton, of Hopemont;

To Mr. and Mrs. E. Stewart James, of Cappahosic House;

To Mr. and Mrs. Chandler Bates, of Airville;

To General and Mrs. R. E. Starr, of Starr Lynn;

To Mr. and Mrs. E. Wright Noble, of Church Hill;

To Mr. and Mrs. George Kirkmeyer, of Kingston Hall;

To Miss Eleanor Perrin, of Goshen;

To Mrs. George Upton, of Poplar Grove;

To Mr. and Mrs. Matthew Fontaine Werth, of Dunham Massie;

To Colonel and Mrs. John Holcombe, of Newstead;

To Mr. and Mrs. William Ashby Jones III, of Ditchly;

To Mr. and Mrs. Stanley Crockett, of Warner Hall;

To Mr. and Mrs. John Maxwell, of Hesse;

To Mr. and Mrs. J. W. C. Cattlett, of Timberneck;

To Dr. George Carneal, of Eagle Point;

To Mr. and Mrs. James Ervin, of Sherwood;

To Mr. and Mrs. George Cunningham, of White Hall;

To The Wellfords, of Glen Roy;

To The Masons, of Wareham;

To The Dabneys, of Exchange;

To The Janneys, of Roaring Springs;

To The Pages, of Shelly;

To Dr. and Mrs. H. E. Thomas, of Gloucester;

To Mrs. Alfred Bell, of Gloucester;

To The Moormans, of Midlothian;

To The Hutchesons, of Fiddler's Green;

To The Kings, of Pig Hill;

To Major and Mrs. W. Milner Gibson, of Colraine;

To Mr. and Mrs. John Warren Cooke, of Mathews;

To Mary K. Spotswood, (Mrs. J. B. Spotswood), of Wicomico, Gloucester County.

Also:

To Mr. Paul Titlow, Editor of the Gloucester-Mathews Gazette Journal;

To the staff of Richmond Newspapers, Inc., especially Mrs. Marjorie Burrell Gratiot and Mr. Earl Jones;

To the staff of the Virginia State Library, especially Eudora Elizabeth Thomas, Bertie Craig Smith, (Mrs. Pinckney A. Smith), Milton C. Russell, and Martha Winfrey;

APPRECIATION

To the staff of the Richmond Public Library, especially Katherine Throckmorton Taylor, (Mrs. Lewis Taylor), Mary Meacham Gilliam, and Margaret Beauchamp;

To the staff of the Library of Congress, in Washington;

To the staff of the Virginia Historical Society;

To the staff of the Virginia State Chamber of Commerce;

To the staff of the Chamber of Commerce of Charleston, South Carolina;

To Nell Carneal Drew, of Lansdowne;

To The Frary Brothers, who own the Shelter;

To Lloyd N. Emory, of Waverly;

To Mr. and Mrs. John L. Lewis, Jr., of Williamsburg, Mrs. F. Snowden Hopkins, of Gloucester, Mr. and Mrs. Catesby G. Jones, of Gloucester, and Miss Mary Kemp, of Richmond;

To the staff of the Book Shop at Miller and Rhoads, Inc., especially Miss Elizabeth O'Neill;

To Miss Lucy Throckmorton, Librarian at the University of Richmond.

Also:

To Ruth Nelson Robins Gordon, (Mrs. Thomas C. Gordon); Janie Schoen Venable, (Mrs. A. Reid Venable); Parke Rouse; John Francis Speight; P. Franklin Tuck; Cornelia Scott Tuck; Franklin Farrar; Virginius Dabney; George Scheer; Marie Sowers; Emma Craddock; Grace Branch; Jane Spence; Bessie Crumpler; Elizabeth Crone Pitts; Mary Cabell Crenshaw; Mr. and Mrs. Lee Hines, Jr.; Mr. and Mrs. Harry Fleshman; Mr. and Mrs. Nimrod Ferguson; Mr. and Mrs. John J. Farrar; Mrs. Huestis Cook; Mr. and Mrs. Theodore R. Martin; Mr. and Mrs. Ellis Berry; Mr. and Mrs. Thomas Hubbard; Clifford Dowdey; Miss Etta Munford; William E. Ellyson, Jr.; Mrs. Fred Brown; Emily Major; Miss Hardy; Susan Seddon Taliaferro Wellford Marshall (Mrs. Thomas R. Marshall); Mr. and Mrs. Beverley Randolph Wellford Marshall; Mr. and Mrs. Laurel Barnett Boyd; Francis Edward Jarvis; Clara Sharpe; Marian Canfield; Annie Hayes O'Neil; The Lane Studio; Harry and Marie Bagby (who take such beautiful photographs), and especially to Teddy Martin, Jr., Franklin Martin, and Martha Lynn Berry.

INTRODUCTION

IN the new Rand-McNally Atlas, the Map of Virginia shows the entire area of the Mobjack Bay country as covering a space about an inch square. In our treatment of "Old Virginia Houses," which in its entirety will cover the state, we are devoting one-sixth of our time, work and space to this square inch. This is because as an area of early homes, there is no other vicinity that surpasses this section in the number of old houses, or in the continuity of years of occupancy. Here we find history and legend. And it was from here that the frontiers of the state and nation were rolled back.

The Mobjack Bay country consists of the counties of Gloucester and Mathews, whose shores are deeply indented with that arm of the Chesapeake known as the Mobjack Bay, and its four estuaries, the Severn, the Ware, the North and the East Rivers. On the south the borders of the land are washed by the waters of the York, and on the east the vista of vision is lost in distance over the blue Chesapeake itself.

It is certain that in tradition, beauty and glamour, there is no part of the Old Dominion that surpasses this area.

It was here that the ancestors of "The Father of His Country" lived, died and lie buried. It was here, also, that the ancestors of a good percentage of that great company, known as Mr. and Mrs. America, lived and died—or went west.

Many authorities agree that there is not a state in the Union, hardly a city, town or county, that does not have some inhabitant who can truthfully say, "One of my ancestors came from Gloucester County in Virginia." (Mathews was originally a part of Gloucester). No wonder tourists come every year, from all over the country. It is simply a case of returning to the land of their fathers.

Hospitality is a grace that has not been forgotten. Most of the porticoed old mansions have two fronts, so they seem to extend a welcome to the traveler, whether he approaches by water or by land.

The old churches stand open, so the wayfarer may enter and kneel, if he feels so inclined.

This is truly the "Magnolia-Honeysuckle South," a land of roses, of moonlight on the water; of sunny gardens, shady lawns, enormous box; of "noble bays, broad rivers and tall trees;" a "Land of Life Worth Living."

In the halls of the old houses, one hears in fancy the soft strains of violins, the swish of silks, the staccato rhythm of military boots accentuating the flutter of tiny slippers.

With all the romantic beauty and traditional charm of this part of the state, there is one sad thing, one grim thing, that impresses us, grieves us, and tears our hearts, as we go from family burying-ground to quiet churchyard. On almost all the old tombs, there is so little span, too little span, between dates of birth and death. A girl "of greatest beauty, gentlest spirit, and quiet demeanor" would have lived, loved, been married, have borne several children, died and been buried, all before she had passed her early twenties.

Many little children, sometimes several in one family, would have died at tender ages. Men would have served in His Majesty's Council, or the House of Burgesses; built homes, married two wives, raised large families, built houses for their sons, yet died before fifty.

All this tells the tragic story of the lack of medical care, of pestilence, or other misfortunes, which harried the early settlers.

Destiny, however, keeps an even balance, or sometimes presses down a measure for posterity. So, perhaps to compensate for her grim record of early deaths shown by the dates on the old tombstones, Gloucester has evened up matters by giving the world a man whose work has saved thousands of lives, Walter Reed, who discovered the cause of yellow fever. His birthplace is now a shrine not far from Belroi.

HISTORY

WHEN the three little boats, the Sarah Constant, the Goodspeed, and the Discovery tied up to the trees at Jamestown that day in May, 1607, and the first English settlers of the new world stepped ashore, to fall on their knees in thanks to God, already the gardens and fields of what is now Gloucester County were planted with the food crops that would sustain these settlers, and prevent their starvation.

At Werowocomoco, north of the York, about twenty-five miles from the confluence of the Mattaponi and the Pamunkey, and in all probability on the site of Shelly, was the seat of the great King Powhatan, who became the ancestor of many prominent Virginians of the white race through the marriage of his daughter, the Princess Pocahontas, to John Rolfe.

It was to Werowocomoco that John Smith was taken as a prisoner, and where he was about to be killed, when, in one of the most dramatic episodes of history, his life was saved by Pocahontas. It was to this place that Smith sent the Dutch to build the wooden house with the marl chimney for Powhatan.

Here Powhatan was crowned by the English, this being the only occasion of the crowning of a king in Virginia, or in the United States, for that matter.

John Ratcliff and a party of thirty went to Werowocomoco in 1609, to negotiate for food. He was not as fortunate as Smith. He and all but two of the party were killed. One was saved by Pocahontas, and the other escaped into the forest.

Sir Thomas Dale burned Werowocomoco in 1612.

There have been many conjectures as to the name of Mobjack. There is a story that, when the sailors called out over the waters of the Bay, the echo would come back from the thick forests along the shore. They said the Bay would mock Jack (the sailor). Then "Mobjack" probably was a corruption of "Mock Jack."

It is not easy to get a continuity of history in Gloucester, for the records have been destroyed three times: first, at the time of Bacon's Rebellion, and the burning of Jamestown in 1676; second, when the Clerk's Office burned in 1820; and third, on the occasion of the evacuation and burning of Richmond in 1865, where the records had been sent for safe-keeping.

In 1634 Virginia was divided into eight shires, the Pamaunkee Shire including the Mobjack Bay country. Then in 1652, the shires were divided into counties, Charles River County including Mobjack.

Owing to the danger from Indians, witness the terrible massacres of 1622 and 1644, there had not been during this early period a great deal of expansion of settlement, but after a treaty with the beloved Necotowance, who had succeeded the cruel Opecancanough, there was never any more widespread trouble with the Indians in Tidewater Virginia. This treaty was made on the fifth of October, 1646, and permitted the Indians to live and hunt on the north side of the York. While there had been many hunting expeditions and temporary camps made by the whites in the Mobjack Bay area, and land grants had been made to some, it was not until 1649 that Gloucester was really opened to the public for settlement. It is probable that the parish churches were organized very soon after this.

From the records in Richmond which were copied from the English Public Record Office, we find that the earliest land grant was in 1635, to Augustine Warner. In 1642 Thomas Curtis, John Jones, Hugh Gwynne and Richard Wyatt took up tracts; James Whiting, in 1643; John Robins, in 1645; Thomas Seawell in 1646; Lewis Burwell and George Reade in 1648; Richard Kemp and Francis Willis in 1649; John Smith, Henry Singleton and William Armistead in 1650; John Page and Thomas Todd in 1653.

Later on came James Rowe, John Thomas, Robert Taliaferro, William Wyatt, William Haywood, Henry Corbell, Anne Bernard, John Lewis, Thomas Graves, Lawrence Smith, John Chapman, George Billups, Charles Roane, William Thornton, Thomas Walker, John Buckner, Philip Lightfoot, William Humphrey, John Tompkins, Robert Peyton, John Fox, Ben Clements, Symond Stubblefield, Robert Pryor, Peter Beverley, John Stubbs, Mordecai Cooke, Humphrey Tabb.

A little later came Thrustons, Roots, Throckmortons, Nicolsons, Vanbibbers, Pages, Byrds, Corbins, Ennises, Dickens, Roys and Smarts.

Home building along the rivers, (for there were no roads), began in earnest, and it was then that the beginnings of houses now standing, or their

xxiv

predecessors on the same sites, were erected. Small houses were built, and later additions made. Still later, alterations, reconstructions and restorations have been undertaken. The houses of Gloucester of the 1950's have evolved through a period of three hundred years, and that evolution is a fascinating study.

Tyndall's Point, where Argoll Yeardley patented 4000 acres of land in 1640, began to be a town, which later was called Gloucester Towne (now Gloucester Point). As early as 1667 there was a fort there.

In 1676 Augustine Warner was Speaker of the House of Burgesses. It was also in 1676 that Bacon's Rebellion extended to the shores of this area, and the body of the leader now enriches the soil of Gloucester, or, perhaps, rests beneath the waters of the York.

Mr. Paul Titlow, Editor of the *Gloucester-Mathews Gazette-Journal* says of Gloucester, "Three wars have been fought on its lawns and fed from its fields." But the sons of Gloucester have fought in nine wars—if one includes the Korean engagement.

From 1607 to 1624 Virginia was ruled by Council (appointed by the London Company), with the House of Burgesses, and a Governor. From 1624 to 1776 Virginia was a Royal Province, ruled by the King's Council (the members of which were appointed by the King, after being recommended by the Governor), with the House of Burgesses and Governor. Many prominent members of the King's Council were from Gloucester. A large number of men from this county also served in the House of Burgesses.

Gloucester men who served on the King's Council were:

George Reade, 1657;
Augustine Warner, I, 1660;
John Pate, 1670;
Augustine Warner, II, of Warner Hall, 1677;
Matthew Kemp, 1681;
John Armistead, 1688;
Henry Whiting, 1690;
Matthew Page, of Timberneck, 1699;
Lewis Burwell, of Carter's Creek, 1702;
John Smith, 1704;
John Lewis, I, of Warner Hall, 1704;
Robert Porteus, of Newbottle, 1713;
Mann Page, of Rosewell, 1714;
Peter Beverley, 1719;
Lewis Burwell, of Carter's Creek, 1744;
John Lewis, II, of Warner Hall, 1748;
John Page, of North End, 1768;

John Page, II, of Rosewell, 1773.

Members of the House of Burgesses from Gloucester were:

Hugh Gwynne,		Nathaniel Burwell,	
Francis Willis,	1652	Ambrose Dudley,	1710;
Abraham Iversonn,		Peter Beverley,	
Richard Pate,	1653;	Ambrose Cooke,	1714;
Thomas Bremen,		Henry Willis,	
Wingfield Webb,	1654;	Thomas Buckner,	1718;
Thomas Ramsey,	1655-56;	Henry Willis,	
Lt. Col. Anthony Elliott,		Nathaniel Burwell,	1720-22;
Capt. Thomas Ramsey,	1657-58;	Giles Cook,	1722;
Capt. Francis Willis,		Giles Cook,	
Capt. Augustine Warner,	1658-59;	Henry Willis,	1723-26;
Capt. Francis Willis,		Francis Willis,	
Capt. Peter Jennings,		Lawrence Smith,	1727-36;
Peter Knight,		Beverley Whiting,	
David Cant,	1659-60;	Francis Willis,	1740;
Capt. Peter Jennings,		Beverley Whiting,	
Capt. Thomas Walker,	1663;	Lewis Burwell,	1742;
Ajt. Gen. Peter Jenyngs,		Beverley Whiting,	
Capt. Thomas Walker,	1666;	Samuel Buckner,	1744;
Col. John Armistead,	1685;	Beverley Whiting,	
Capt. James Ransom,		Francis Willis,	1745-49;
John Baylor,	1693;	Beverley Whiting,	
James Ransone,		John Page,	1752-54;
Mordecai Cooke,	1696-97;	John Page,	
Peter Beverley, Speaker,		Thomas Whiting,	1755-68;
Mordecai Cooke,	1702;	Thomas Whiting,	
Peter Beverley, Speaker,	1706;	Lewis Burwell,	1759-75;
Peter Beverley,			

The Delegates of the Conventions of 1775, 1776, were Thomas Whiting and Lewis Burwell.

After the outrages at Williamsburg, the gunpowder plot, and other incidents that led Virginia to join in the rebellion against Britain, Lord Dunmore began his ravaging depredations along the Bay Coast. He landed on Gwynn's Island—with the British fleet near by. The Virginian forces under General Andrew Lewis attacked the fleet, forcing it to withdraw, taking Dunmore along; he never returned. This was the end of Royal government in Virginia and happened July 9, 1776.

Towards the end of the Revolution the scene of activity shifted again to Gloucester. Cornwallis had troops all around Yorktown and in Gloucester. Virginia militia with French forces under Choisy assisted by the cavalry of the Duke de Lauzun had an active engagement with Tarleton's cavalry forces, which ended in British withdrawal. A few days later when Cornwallis found himself bottled up at Yorktown, he planned to cross the York into Gloucester, hoping thus to escape, but a storm prevented his doing so, and he had to surrender on October 19, 1781.

The militia of the county during the Revolution were under Colonel Sir John Peyton, with Lt. Colonel Thomas Whiting, Major Thomas Boswell and Lt. Warner Lewis on his staff. Other officers who served in the Revolution were:

Captains:

John Billups, Richard Billups, George Booth, William Buckner, John Camp, Jasper Clayton, Gibson Cheverius, John Dixon, John Hubard, Richard Matthews, Robert Matthews, Benjamin Shackelford, William Smith, John Whiting and John Willis.

Lieutenants were:

Churchill Armistead, James Baytop, James Bentley, John Billups, Thomas Buckner, Dudley Cary, Samuel Cary, John Foster, Robert Gayle, George Green, Richard Hall, Hugh Hayes, Edward Matthews, William Sears, Phillip Tabb.

Ensigns:

Thomas Baytop, William Bentley, Peter Bernard, Richard Davis, William Davis, Samuel Eddins, Josiah Foster, John Fox, John Gale, Christopher Garland, John Hayes, William Haywood, James Laughlin, George Plummer, Henry Stevens, Thomas Tabb.

Major General William Boothe Taliaferro tells in an article in the *William and Mary Quarterly Review* of remembering that his father told of watching the British fleet in the York River, during the War of 1812, when his father (Warner Taliaferro) was a young boy. He said his father watched the fleet from the porch at Airville. It is a matter of record that the fleet committed unpleasant incursions from time to time along the coast. The militia were called up for defense, and were under the command of Colonel William Jones. His staff consisted of Capt. Catesly Jones, Capt. Baytop, and Capt. Richard Jones of The Cottage.

Colonel Scaife Whiting had command of the Gloucester Horse, and served outside of the county.

In the Clerk's Office at Gloucester there is a complete roster of the officers and men of the county who served in the Confederacy. Reading these names is like reading the rolls of the old parishes. They are the same names, the same families.

During the Civil War the women did their part, too.

After the Civil War, as Sally Nelson Robins so neatly puts it, "The pride which the sons of the old land-owners took in being scions of Cavaliers, and fathers of the Union is changed into this glory, 'My father was a Confederate Soldier.'"

From then on Gloucester has lifted up her head, and in spite of the struggles and losses she had just endured she kept pressing forward. Progress has continued. Northern money, and, yes, Southern money too, have combined with aristocratic blood and patriotic courage, to make this area one of culture and prosperity. Since the turn of this century the cultivation of tobacco has gradually given place to the cultivation of flowers and the raising of beef cattle.

The public libraries of both counties are kept up-to-date, and privately owned libraries are becoming larger and of wider scope in subject matter than of yore.

Never in the history of the Mobjack Bay country have the homes been more beautifully kept, more artistically and tastefully furnished, nor more comfortable to live in than now, in the 1950's. Up-to-date utilities and modern gadgets; late model cars and excellent roads; motor boats, daily papers, television, radio, telephones and airplanes all combine to make the Mobjack Bay country as convenient a place to live in as any part of the country. The excellent gardens, the nearby rivers, quick transportation and the innovation of the "deep freeze" unite to provide even more sumptuous tables than those so famous in the good old days. In fact, the residents of Gloucester and Mathews no longer need to reminisce about the "grandeur that was;" they may freely revel in the grandeur that is again.

THE OLD HOMES
IN THE 1950's

IN *Old Churches, Ministers and Families of Virginia*, Bishop Meade wrote of the homes of the Gloucester-Mathews area during the 1850's. Almost fifty years later, Mrs. Sally Nelson Robins gave some account of these same houses in her delightful little book, *History of Gloucester County, Virginia, and Its Families*. Then in 1915, Mr. Robert Lancaster gave an even fuller account of the homes in this section, naming owners, and showing illustrations in his extensive work, *Historic Virginia Homes and Churches*.

All these books are out of print. Edith Tunis Sale's books are also out of print. The demand of the public for descriptions, pictures, information as to the lives of owners, in fact any information available concerning these old houses, has been so great, that I feel impelled to present to the best of my ability a picture of the old houses as they are now, in the 1950's, together with the history, the various reconstructions, restorations and remodelings of these houses, as well as legend and tradition about them. Some have changed hands many times—others not so often. Some of the houses have vanished, but because they are so intertwined with the early life of this section, mention is made of them.

Although this work is presented more or less from the viewpoint of these charming old houses as homes, their architecture has been a fascinating study too. It has its own characteristic style which has, of course, been subjected to many influences that inevitably have given direction to its evolution. In many cases it is difficult to say just where the "old" part of the house ends and the "new" begins. The most definite influences represented are Georgian, Dutch Colonial, Palladian and Greek Revival.

Little England land front. Wing to right is older part.

PART ONE
ON THE YORK

THE natural eminence of the terrain along the banks of the York provided desirable homesites and led to the building of many beautiful mansions overlooking the broad blue waters of the York river. In the July 1894 issue of the *William and Mary Quarterly*, the Editor, in some notes, remarks that down the York from Porteus Mansion there had been well-built brick houses about every mile, and at the time he wrote, some few still survived. He mentions the families which lived along the river in years gone by, and used it as a travel route to visit back and forth. Those included in his list were the Smiths, of Purton; the family of Capt. John Stubbs, of Cappahosic; the Burwells, of Carter's Creek; the Warners, of Warner Hall; the Pages, of Rosewell; the Manns, of Timberneck, and the Perrins, of Sarah's Creek.

LITTLE ENGLAND

THE mansion nearest the mouth of the river, and situated on Sarah's Creek, is Little England, formerly called Sarah's Creek House.

From "Observations in Several Voyages and Travels in America in the Year 1736" from the *London Magazine* of July 1746, in a discussion of excellent harbors on the Eastern Coast of Virginia, we find mention made of the "Harbor of Men of War, in which is Sarah's Creek."

John Perrin, aged twenty-one, sailed from London in 1635 (Hotten's "Emigrants"). Entered in the Court proceedings of the York records for 1648

1

was found an undated letter from his mother to John Perrin, the immigrant. It reads:

"Son John: My love to yo', and I was very glad to heare of yo' health, but very sorry to heare of ye' accident wch befell yo' by fire. I have sent yo a boy wch I desire that you would have as much care of as if he was yo owne alsoe. I have sent yo some things, so much as I am able at this tyme, and if God shall enable me to live another yeare I shall send yo more. Ye father hath departed this life, and hath left you a little house in ye south-gate streete in burg worth the matter of 40 lb., there is a note in ye barrell it lieth at ye topp in ye new blankett, and I have sent you by Tho; a small piece of gould for your wife alsoe I have pd for ye boy his passage, his name is Backer Yo' Uncle Christopher lives at Ascamack at Cheryston Creeke,

As yo desire my blessing have a care of ye boy, and learn him his trade, and not to pt from him. . . . my love to you an yo' wife desiring of God to keepe. . . .

Your loveing mother Susan Perrin"

This letter would indicate that the Perrin family was one of integrity as well as ability, and certainly this mother-in-law displayed a high degree of tact in sending her daughter-in-law a "small piece of gould."

The grant for the land was dated April 1651 and embraced 400 acres. It was deeded to John Perrin by Governor Berkeley, for transportation into the colony. (Evidently John Perrin brought over several immigrants with him.)

There are several graves at Sarah's Creek. The inscription on one tomb is

Here Lyeth Ye Body of
Mrs. Mary Perrin Daughter
of Mr. John and Mrs. Mary
Perrin died Sep^br Ye 18th
1738 Aged three years
One month and five days.

This must have been the great grand-daughter of John the immigrant. There is another tombstone the inscription of which reads

Here lies the Body of
John Perrin Son of Thomas
and Elizabeth Perrin

Little England from corner of the garden.

Little England river front. Home of Mr. and Mrs. Theodore Pratt.

Who departed this life
Nov^br 2d 1752
Aged 63 Years 1 Month
and 2 Days.

Thomas, son of the original John, and Elizabeth raised their family of six during the last fifteen years of the seventeenth century:

Elizabeth baptized in February 25, 1686.
Mary baptized April last 1688.
John, September 21, 1690 (Capt. John Perrin of Sarah's Creek).
Susannah baptized March 2, 1698.

Little England showing new bath house and swimming pool.

Catherine Xber 30, 1700.
Isaac baptized February 26, 1702 (buried September 2, 1733).

Their descendants married into many old families.

Sarah's Creek was named for Sarah the Duchess of Marlborough.

On July 16, 1781 in a communication from Capt. Samuel Eddins to Governor Nelson is this message:

"A Pilot Boat from Gloucester Town seized some time ago by order of the Baron, belonging to a gentleman in Maryland is sunk in Sarah's Creek, and might be sold advantageously."

Staircase in great hall at Little England.

In 1781 Brigadier-General Weeden mentions the Perrin House in a letter to Washington. In this letter he reported: "I have a lay of Horsemen from Perrin's House to Camp. The House stands at the mouth of Sarah's Creek and commands a full view of Gloster and York and all their shipping." This "lay of horsemen" were experienced French hussars from the legion of Lauzun which had arrived in America with the army of Rochambeau. Lauzun, popular at the Court of Versailles, and believed to be a lover of Marie Antoinette, was the first to announce the surrender of Cornwallis to Louis XVI.

Lookouts in the Perrin House kept the commanders advised of enemy operations in the York River.

During the War of 1812 Little England became a hospital for wounded soldiers. In the *Virginia Historical Magazine* in a discussion of the Perrin

Living room at Little England.

family, there is a description of Little England as it was early this century. It reads:

> "In Gloucester County, at the mouth of the York River, opposite Yorktown, the old Perrin Mansion is still standing in good condition. It is in the style of architecture so usual in Virginia during the reigns of the Georges, a large brick building two stories high, and four rooms on each floor, wainscoted and panelled. The house is in full view of Yorktown, at the mouth of Sarah's Creek, on the east side of Gloucester Point."

Little England was built in 1716 by Capt. John Perrin, (son of Thomas and

Dining room at Little England.

8

Dining room mantel, at Little England.

Elizabeth Perrin). The plans were said to have been made by Sir Christopher Wren. There is a frame wing (early Colonial), with gables, which was built before 1690. It was in this building that Thomas and Elizabeth raised their family. In the main building there is a grand central hall with one huge room on each side. The large windows in these rooms open to both fronts. The brasses on the doors of both fronts are original, and the superb staircase leads to the second floor, where the floor plan of the first floor is repeated.

The paneling in the hall and the great rooms is beautiful, the color tone being a delightful pale green. Williamsburg Restoration representatives have conferred with Mr. and Mrs. Theodore Pratt, the present owners of Little England, concerning this color tone which has been declared the truest of the colonial decorative colors.

Inside the mansion, which Mr. and Mrs. Pratt have restored to its original beauty, one finds exquisite antiques and priceless paintings. There is a Rembrandt Peale over the mantel in the dining room. It is of General George Washington. Here we also find a Daubigny, a Bonheur, and a Monticelli, and other paintings.

In the living room there is a magnificent Waterford glass chandelier, and in the dining room the chandelier has a center of deep purple Bristol glass and gallery of gilt with tear-drop crystals.

The grounds spread out in great stretches of grass with enormous quantities of box, cedars, crepe myrtles, and trees of different varieties. Adjoining are flower and vegetable gardens, and beyond, endless fields of priceless daffodils. In the spring these blossoms turn the fields to stripes of green and gold.

Down where the lawn meets the river, Mr. and Mrs. Pratt have built a large swimming pool, and a modern bathhouse, complete with a big fireplace in the lounge, and showers in the wings.

TIMBERNECK

THE ample rambling old mansion known as Timberneck Hall stands on the York River, opposite Ringfield, and not far from Powhatan's Chimney, which was built for Powhatan by Capt. John Smith. The mansion was built by the first John Catlett in the county, probably in 1776, and is now the house of Mr. and Mrs. John W. C. Catlett, who are of the fifth generation descendants of the first John. This house of frame construction, in Georgian style, superseded an earlier house, also known as Timberneck Hall, which was on land granted to George Minifye. In the latter half of the seventeenth century it was the home of John Mann, the immigrant, and Mary, his wife. Their daughter, Mary, only child and heiress, was born at Timberneck in 1672. She was

Timberneck Hall front view.

married to Matthew Page, son of Sir John Page, of Williamsburg, and for some years they lived at Timberneck with her parents.

Practically all trace of the original Timberneck house is gone. Almost a hundred years ago Bishop Meade visited the scene. He refers to the place as "Mr. Catlett's farm." "In, or near the stable yard, in an open place," he found tombstones lying around, or piled on each other. According to one of these tombstones, Matthew and Mary Page buried a daughter, Elizabeth, aged three years, here. She died March 15, 1693.

John Mann, and Mary, his wife, were buried here. He died January 7,

11

Timberneck Hall side rear view.

1694—aged sixty-three. She died March 1703-4—aged fifty-six.

When John Mann died, his name died with him, but his daughter named her son Mann, and among his descendants, particularly the Pages, the name has been used every generation, for more than two hundred years.

Part of John Mann's vast acres passed to his daughter, and on to her descendants, the Pages. But part of the estate went to the Catletts, descendants of John Mann's wife's children by her first husband, Edmund Berkeley, of Gloucester County.

12

In a letter from Mr. John W. C. Catlett, of Timberneck Hall, to Mrs. H. O. Sanders under date of January 29, 1951, he says in part:

"I have before me a copy of the original 'Land Grant,' taken from Patent Book I, page 704 in the Land Office at Richmond.

"'To all whom these presents shall come I, Sir Francis Wyatt Lt. Governor and Captain Generall of Virginia, etc., etc. By Instructions from the Kings Most Excellent Magestie directed me and the Councell of State etc., etc., Give and grant unto George Minifye Esq., Three thousand acres to start at the creeke upon the west side of the Indians feilds, opposite to Queene's Creeke and extends down the river to a creeke called by the name of Timber Necke Creeke Eastward.'"

Mr. Catlett continues by saying:

"This is by order of Court bearing date the Eleventh of October Anno 1639, and was given for 'transportation at his own ppr costs and charges of sixtie pons to the Colony.' Mr. Minifye was a member of the 'Councell of State'. . . .

"This three thousand acres is supposed to have included Rosewell. . . .

"I don't know anything about the original house. This house [the present home of the Catletts], we have been told, was built by the first John Catlett, who came here, according to Cousin Merriweather Jones, in 1776. . . .

"The present Timberneck house was originally 40 x 40 feet, a cellar, two stories and an attic. Three large chimneys, two of them running all the way from the cellar. The cellar, seven feet pitch; the rooms on the first floor, ten feet pitch, actual measure; and the second floor eight feet. The dining room sixteen by twenty-one feet—the parlor a little larger. The house is frame.

"There are two places an older house could have been. There is a very distinct old foundation we have plowed into, an hundred, twenty-five yards East of the house, and my wife thinks she has found one in the flower garden in front of the house.

"The original [present] Catlett house, had seven rooms. Grandpa added three and a hall in 1856. The original had a hall on the north end too.

"Some of the names Minifye brought to the colony were Pixlry, Greene, Chapman, Martin, Burgis, Ward, Prince, Sheers, Turner, Gauett, Sharples, Sherbourne Williams, William Jones, Wilkinson

13

Rosewell from an old photograph taken by H. P. Cook in the 1870s.

Kennon, Richards, Hawkins, Mason, Reed, Leech, Powell, Walker.
   "The Assembly acted on this Grant January sixth, 1639 and it was sealed with the 'seale of the Colony at James Cittie the ninth of March 1639.'"

ROSEWELL

MATTHEW PAGE and his wife, Mary, daughter of John Mann, moved from Timberneck to a "simple wooden structure" on a high promontory on the York, not far from Timberneck. This was to be the site of Rosewell. The exact date of their moving is not on record, but according to the tombstones at Rosewell, Matthew Page died the 9th of January, 1703, aged forty-five, and Mary died March 24, 1707 in her thirty-sixth year.

Before August, 1704, three of their young children, Matthew, Mary, and Ann were buried here.

Mann Page was the only child who survived his mother. With the inheritance from both parents, he was a very wealthy man. His first wife was Judith, daughter of Ralph Wormeley. After her death, he married Judith, daughter of Robert Carter. In 1725 he started building Rosewell.

Overlooking the York River, and Carter's Creek, this mansion (in the style of a Georgian town house), was four stories high, including the basement, and had two turrets on the roof, inside of which were little rooms. These had windows on the four sides, and made excellent look-outs.

Built of red brick, in Flemish bond, and with marble lintels, and other elaborate masonry trim, Rosewell was the finest house in America. The carved staircases, mantels and paneling were said to have been exquisite beyond description. The entrance hall had full-height pilasters. Sally Nelson Robins says eight people could ascend the great staircase abreast. The balustrade of the stairs was carved with designs of baskets of fruits and flowers. But Mann Page did not live to finish his work. In 1730 he died, and the magnificent home he was building for joyful celebrations became a house of sorrow and death.

Mr. Page's son, Mann Page II, completed the house, but there were many difficulties in the way, and he was compelled to ask to have certain entails on property left by his father lifted, before he could pay his father's debts and continue work on the mansion. It was about 1744 before it was finished.

Mann II married, first, Miss Alice Grymes, daughter of the Honorable John Grymes of Middlesex; and second, Miss Ann Corbin Tayloe. John Page, a son of the first marriage, became Governor of Virginia. He was a close friend of Thomas Jefferson. They were in college at William and Mary together. They both went courting in the Burwell family. Mr. Page was successful, and married Miss Fanny Burwell (a cousin of the Carter's Creek Burwells). Mr. Jefferson, however, was refused the hand of the lovely Miss Rebecca, of Carter's Creek, and his heart was temporarily broken.

Governor John Page was a brilliant man and a great leader. He was simple in his tastes, however, and entertained large numbers of friends with an ease and simplicity that made them feel an everyday at-homeness at Rosewell. Mr. Jefferson used to visit him for days, and it has been said that he wrote the draft for the Declaration of Independence in one of the turret rooms on the roof of Rosewell. It was on this roof that the first weather bureau in America was put in operation. John Page died in 1808.

15

In 1838 the vast Rosewell estate passed from the Page family. It was bought by a Mr. Booth, who paid $12,000 for it. He sold $35,000 worth of cedars, bricks, wainscoting, etc.—and received $22,000 for the place. Alterations and modernization took place, presumably during his ownership.

The deck-on-hip roof was changed to low hip, and pediments were added to the end pavilions. West and East dependencies were built, but were later removed.

(According to an insurance policy, a brick stable 24 by 120 feet had been built in 1802).

In 1855 Rosewell became the home of the Deans, who were charming gracious people. They made the mansion again a center of society. One of the Dean daughters was married to Judge Fielding Lewis Taylor and they made their home here.

In 1916 the mansion was burned.

Before the wings were removed, there were within the walls of Rosewell thirty-five rooms, three wide halls, and nine passageways.

Mr. Thomas Tileston Waterman, the distinguished architect, says that even in ruins the walls of Rosewell show a fineness in construction not equaled elsewhere in America.

SHELLY

SHELLY, long the home of the Pages, is near the York. It adjoins Rosewell, and was originally a part of it. The name was derived from the great quantities of shells all about the place. It is known to have been a center of great celebration among the Indians, and is probably the site of Werowocomoco, Powhatan's capital.

Elizabeth Nelson, daughter of General Thomas B. Nelson, married Mann Page and for a long time made her home at Shelly. In 1827 Julia Randolph was married to Thomas N. Page, of Shelly. They became the parents of the noted author, Thomas Nelson Page, of Oakland, Hanover County.

In her last days, Elizabeth Nelson Page (Mrs. Mann Page), wrote down many interesting memories of her earlier life at Shelly. In a letter to the Honorable H. A. Wise, of Washington, D. C., of December 1, 1837, she writes of the sacrifices made by her father of health, life and fortune. She says, "He never had a day's health after the siege at Yorktown."

Shelly is still in the Page family. Mr. Mann Page, the present owner, tells us that the original house, built in the eighteenth century, was burned some time after the Civil War. He says that it was a two-part frame building, with dormer windows, large chimneys and two outside entrances.

The present house is of frame construction, with center hall, and rooms

16

on each side. There are two stories; and before some of them were closed up, there were fireplaces in all rooms. The rooms are large, and the woodwork good. Most of the old garden is gone, but there remains some fine boxwood. This, the present house, was built in 1885.

CARTER'S CREEK

THE early home of the Burwell family, sometimes called Fairfield, was architecturally unique. The main building had two wings extending back at right angles. One of the wings was demolished or burned in early years. In the other was the ballroom.

The basement had a vault in the center, built of bricks, which probably was used to store valuables. The ceiling of the basement was supported by brick arches.

The chimneys were of interesting treatment, being somewhat similar to those at Bacon's Castle. Fairfield, or Carter's Creek, as it was later called, was near Rosewell.

Lewis Burwell, the immigrant, married Lucy Higginson, only child of Captain Robert Higginson, early commander in Indian wars. It was to this Lewis that 2350 acres of land were granted in 1648. He died in 1658, having lived in York County most of his married life. Some authorities say he may have built Fairfield, but dates and records seem to point to the son, Lewis II, as the builder, at least of the main part.

There was the date 1692 in iron figures, in one gable. The iron letters L A B were also built into the wall. Lewis Burwell II's wife was Abigail, niece and heiress of President of the Council, Nathaniel Bacon.

Their son, Nathaniel, inherited the estate at the death of his father in 1710. (Abigail had died in 1672.) Nathaniel married Elizabeth, daughter of Robert Carter. Their son was Lewis Burwell III (1710-1752).

He attended Cambridge University, and became President of the Council and Acting Governor of Virginia.

His daughter, Rebecca, after refusing the hand of Mr. Thomas Jefferson, became the wife of Mr. Jacqueline Ambler. They had several beautiful daughters, who were great belles. One of them, Mary Willis Ambler, became the wife of Chief Justice John Marshall, of Richmond.

Lewis Burwell IV was educated at Eton and Inns of Court, but when the Revolution came, his sympathies were with America. He married Judith, daughter of Mann Page II, and they had many descendants.

It was during his lifetime that Carter's Creek passed from the Burwell family.

For a good many years Carter's Creek was the home of the Thrustons.

Carter's Creek (Fairfield).

Thomas Waterman mentions in *Mansions of Virginia* an unusual urn at Timberneck Hall. He says the bowl of the urn was carved with baroque bas-relief ornament of leafage, and a grotesque monkey's head. This came from Fairfield (Carter's Creek), and was probably a central finial of the mantel—or one of a pair of crossettes.

Although the mansion burned many years ago, traces of the foundations of the house, and of the dependencies may still be found.

In 1930 the land on which the house stood was bought by J. W. Lambert, wealthy yachtsman, of St. Louis, who was a descendant of the Burwell family.

CAPPAHOSIC HOUSE

UP the river a mile from the mouth of Carter's Creek was the wharf of Cappa-

Cappahosic House.

hosack. The first time this name was found in American history was in 1608 when it was shown on a chart sent to England with Captain Smith's "News from Virginia." At least this chart was found in the Spanish Archives, and is generally conceded to be the one which was sent to England in 1608. At that time Cappahosack was an Indian village on the York, and Powhatan offered to make Captain Smith "King of Cappahosack" for the price of "two great guns and a grindstone."

There has been a great deal of discussion about the meaning of the name, variously spelled in the old days when spelling was subject to personal whimsey—Cappahosac, Capahowsick and Cappahosic. William Wallace Tooker, an authority on Indian names, says that it is the Natick Kuppoho-we-es-et,— "at, or near the place of shelter," "a haven," "covert," or "woods." The main stem means to stop or close up.

19

From the *Calendar of State Papers* we find transportation at the site by ferry, in 1706. "From Capt. Mathew's to Cappohofack—the price for a man fifteen pence, for a man and horse, two shillings and six pence, etc., etc."

Thomas Buckner kept the Ferry sometime in the eighteenth century.

From "Laws of Virginia under George II" we find that in October 1748 the price for crossing the Ferry was one shilling, three pence, each, for horse and man.

In the *Virginia Gazette* under date of March 28, 1751, we find:

"The subscriber, having undertaken to keep the Ferry at Capahosack, gives Notice, That the said Ferry for the future shall be kept in the best manner, having provided a good Boat, and a sufficient Number of Hands for that Purpose, and a very large Canoe for putting off Footmen, or such as don't choose to cross with the Horses. Also keeps a Public House at the said Ferry, where all Gentlemen may be well accommodated, and depend on meeting with all possible Dispatch in crossing the said Ferry and on making a Smoake on the other side of the River, The Boat will be immediately sent over.'
Signed
William Thornton."

Cappahosic House itself was built in 1712 by Captain John Stubbs, who had patented the land of the Cappahosic tract in 1652 and in 1702. The austere simplicity of the architecture makes for classical beauty in the finished product.

The house (early Georgian) is almost square, with a hall in the center; with four rooms downstairs, and four rooms upstairs. In each of these eight rooms there is a corner fireplace. The two huge chimneys, each with four flues, are built to the front of the ridge of the roof, for all four front rooms are smaller than those at the back. This arrangement resulted in very unusual roof treatment, inasmuch as the gable ends were clipped. The house is built of red brick which has been covered with white water-proofing cement paint. This not only keeps dampness out, but makes an excellent appearance.

Inside, the glistening of the wide pine floors is reflected in the fine old

ON FACING PAGE

(Above) Dining room at Cappahosic.

(Below) Fireplace in dining room at Cappahosic.

In the drawing room at Cappahosic.

hand-carved mahogany paneling, which in the dining room extends entirely to the ceiling, and in the other rooms to chair rail height. Above the living room mantel the paneling extends to the ceiling. The downstairs ceilings are twelve feet high, and those upstairs, ten. The staircase is unique in its simple beauty.

The Stubbs family lived at Cappahosic House for many years. Later on it was the home of the Baytops. During their residence here the place became known as "Baytop."

In 1947 Mr. and Mrs. E. Stewart James purchased the place, and set

22

Fireplace in the living room at Cappahosic.

about restoring it. This was a tremendous job, for the house had been closed up for several years. However, perseverance won out, and from attic to cellar the restoration is perfect.

At the back there is a later wing which has several bedrooms and a modern kitchen and bath, but the Jameses live in the old part, too. There is an old square grand piano, with a tone like a harpsichord; there are open fires; gleaming antique silver; a tester bed with a crocheted spread; Hogarth prints; and an ancient mariner's compass. The light fixtures are unique. They,

23

Bedroom at Cappahosic, notice the bed steps.

24

and the charm of the iron grill work, and the atmosphere of antiquity, lend the illusion that one is actually living back in the days when Cappahosic House was first built—two hundred and fifty years ago.

The gardens are being restored in the spirit of the age to which the house belonged.

PURTON

UP the river from Cappahosic, in an olden day, was the house known as "Portan," "Poetan" or "Purton." We find many references to this old place. A grant for 1665 acres, dated March 31, 1649, was made to William John Clarke. This land, commonly known as Portan, was bounded by Broad Creek, York River and Tanks Poropotank Creek, or Adams' Creek.

The home in its heyday consisted of two stories and basement with front stoop and back porch. The view to the river was excellent. There must have been a mill near the home, for mention is made of a mill dam.

It was near Purton that some servants who were former soldiers of Cromwell held a rendezvous in 1663 at which they planned a rebellion. One of their number, however, gave away the plot, so they were prevented from carrying it out by the Governor, Sir William Berkeley.

In studying the history of Purton we find references to the Berkeley family, the Bernard family, also the Whaley family; but it is the Smith family which is most frequently identified with Purton. And to be a descendant of the Smiths, of Purton, is almost like being descended from royalty.

Mrs. Stanley Lloyd now owns Purton. She has recently made some additions to the house, and is restoring and enlarging the gardens.

POROPOTANK

NEAR the mouth of Poropotank Creek, on the York, formerly stood a classically-simple, early Georgian old home called Poropotank (now long gone), later known as Violet Banks. This house was said to have been the counterpart of Cappahosic House, and was the home of Edward Porteus. Some say that he planned both houses. It was through his son, Robert Porteus, that Queen Elizabeth II, of England, is claimed to be related to George Washington, Robert E. Lee, and many other distinguished Americans.

There are references in early Virginia history to the Poropotank Warehouses; also to the meeting at John Pate's house, near Poropotank, of the Loyalists, about the time Governor Berkeley's friends rose in Middlesex, during Bacon's Rebellion.

In connection with Poropotank we find many references to the Porteus

25

family, also to the Dudley family, and the Lewis family. Charles Roanes was granted land on Poropotank Creek, possibly adjoining the Porteus property. In his notes, *William and Mary Quarterly*, 1894, the Editor says:

"'Violet Banks' is the modern name of the house of Edward Porteus, the emigrant. It is an old square brick bldg., two stories and a half, with four rooms to the floor. Though abandoned, it still retains the fine panelling and interior carving of the long past. It fronts York River and on the West is Poropotank Creek. Rob't. Porteus, his son, lived at 'New Bottle' subsequently called 'Concord.' In 1693 Edward Porteus was recommended by the Governor of Virginia for appointment to the Council as a 'Gentleman of estate and standing suitable for appointment to Council,' (Sainsbury, Mss.). He was a vestryman of Petsworth Parish in 1681 (vestry book). He married 'The Relict of Robert Lee,' who left in his will 'seven pounds to the poor of Petsworth.'"

Edward Porteus's tomb is at Violet Banks at the mouth of Poropotank Creek.

PART TWO
ON THE SEVERN

WARNER HALL

THE land on which Warner Hall stands was patented by Augustine Warner I (1610-1674), very early in the history of Gloucester. He was Justice of York in 1650, and Justice of Gloucester in 1656. He was the great-great-grandfather of George Washington and through him Robert E. Lee, The Queen Mother of England (1955), and Queen Elizabeth II, are kin. His wife's name was Mary. They lie buried in the graveyard at Warner Hall.

Augustine Warner II (1642-1681) inherited Warner Hall at the death of his father in 1674. He married Mildred Reade, the daughter of George Reade, founder of Yorktown, and after her death, Elizabeth Martian. Augustine II was speaker of the House of Burgesses during Bacon's Rebellion in 1676, and also was a member of the Council.

After the burning of Jamestown, Bacon came over into Gloucester, making Warner Hall his headquarters. It was while here that he invited the "Oath of Fidelity" of his fellow countrymen.

When Augustine Warner II died he left three daughters (his sons having died young). Mary became the wife of John Smith, of Purton, on the York, and their son Augustine Smith was said to have been one of the Knights of the Golden Horseshoe—with Governor Spotswood, on his famous expedition across the Blue Ridge in 1716. Mildred, another daughter of Augustine Warner II, married Lawrence Washington (grandfather of George), of Westmoreland, and her second husband was George Gale. Her three Washington children were John, who built Highgate, Augustine, father of George Washington, and Mildred. Augustine Washington married Mary Ball, and named his son George for his great-grandfather, George Reade, who founded Yorktown.

Warner Hall river front. The home of Mr. and Mrs. Stanley Crockett.

28

The stables at Warner Hall.

Elizabeth, the third daughter of Augustine Warner II, became the wife of John Lewis and inherited Warner Hall. Their son, John Lewis II (1702-1754) was a member of His Majesty's Council, and was prominent in the county. For generations the Lewises lived here, and members of the family emigrated to all parts of the United States. Their descendants built Belle Farm, Eagle Point, Abingdon, and Severn Hall, all in Virginia. Elizabeth and John Lewis I's grandson, Colonel Fielding Lewis, of Belle Farm, married Catherine Washington, and after her death married Elizabeth Washington

29

(better known as Betty), sister of George. He built beautiful Kenmore for her, in Fredericksburg.

In the early part of the nineteenth century Mr. Colin Clarke purchased Warner Hall and continued the tradition of hospitality for which the Hall was so widely known.

Always pretentious and large, Warner Hall was of brick, connected by a brick covered way to the kitchen on the left. Another brick covered way connected the house with the office on the right.

In 1845 the center of the original building was burned, leaving only the two wings—each with a hall and one large room on the first floor, and a quaint platform stairway going up to a hall, and two nice size bedrooms upstairs.

The following is taken from a note written to Mrs. H. O. Sanders (who was Miss Nina Taliaferro), of Gloucester County, by her cousin, Mrs. Martha Page Vandegrift, who died in 1932 at the age of one hundred and two:

> "The old Warner Hall house was burned in 1845. Mr. Colin Clarke who then owned it added to one of the brick offices a brick bungalow in which he lived until his death in the early 60's. The original building had very large rooms—so large was the drawing room that I remember being at a large party there, when a child, and the Clarke boys and Bryan girls and my brother and I had our own cotillion in a corner of the room. In those days neighbor children were invited to the "grown up" parties. Mr. Cheney, when he built the present house, connected it with the brick offices. Warner Hall and Eagle Point were among the anti-bellum houses with many others far famed for their generous hospitality, as has been said, 'every house was a club for guests.' "

After much research we conclude that the main part of the first house on the site was built in 1674, although there may have been a house or a wing on this site earlier in the 17th century; a later house was certainly built about 1740. Several fires in the 18th and 19 centuries took their toll of this structure. But research establishes pretty conclusively that the restorations and additions that have been made have salvaged as much of the original as it was possible to salvage. Today Warner Hall with magnificent center of frame construction having columned fronts towards the land approach, and towards the Severn, and the two brick wings, stands as majestically as ever in its grove of century-old trees.

Its occupants still enjoy the use of some of the original dependencies.

It was sold by Paul T. O'Mally and Herbert I. Lewis in 1946 to I. S. Crockett. Beef cattle are grazed on the large rich fields which border the river.

An original outbuilding at Warner Hall.

31

Eagle Point in the river, from which the place gets its name.

The land of the Warner Hall estate joins that of Eagle Point, which also faces the Severn, and that of White Marsh, which extends to the shores of the Ware.

EAGLE POINT

EAGLE POINT, on the Severn River, was the house of John Randolph Bryan and his wife Elizabeth Tucker Coalter. Mr. Bryan was a namesake of John Randolph, of Roanoke, and was educated under his watchful care.

Elizabeth Coalter was a beloved niece, and the heiress of John Randolph, of Roanoke. When she and Mr. Bryan were married, it seems the combination of their fortunes enabled them to entertain lavishly. However, thirty-two years after their marriage, the gracious hospitality for which Eagle Point was famed, came to an end, due to the outbreak of the Civil War. In 1862 the estate passed from the Bryan family. It was part of the original Warner Hall Grant.

Many years later, the distinguished Mr. Joseph Bryan, publisher and philanthropist, of Richmond, who was born at Eagle Point, bought back the estate. He enlarged and beautified the house, improved the grounds, and re-established its reputation for hospitality. His portrait hangs at the Court-house in Gloucester. It has the following inscription:

"C. S.A. 1862-65
Born at Eagle Point, Gloucester
County, Va. Aug. 13, 1845.
Died at Laburnum, Henrico
Co., Nov. 26, 1908."

Eagle Point is large and handsome, with many gables, columns, chimneys, and porches. The rooms are beautifully and comfortably furnished with a tasteful combination of the modern and the antique.

The name, Eagle Point, derives from a formation of land that juts out into the river. The house is now the home of Dr. George Carneal.

The old family graveyard is on a small island in the Severn River, near the house, and the dead rest in the shade of the pines.

SEVERNBY

SEVERNBY, sometimes called Severn Hall, was originally part of the Eagle Point estate. The present house was built by Mr. Alfred Withers, and is a pleasant home which overlooks the river.

LANSDOWNE

LANSDOWNE, also on the Severn, was long the home of the Thrustons, a prominent family of Gloucester. It was here that Miss Nelson, the charming young daughter of Dr. Wilmer Nelson, came as the bride of Edward Thruston. Lansdowne is now the property of Nell Carneal Drew.

Eagle Point land front.

Eagle Point river front.

A garden spot at White Marsh.

36

PART THREE
ON THE WARE

WHITE MARSH

BACK from the Ware, on the Tidewater Trail in Gloucester, on the original grant of land to the honorable Lewis Burwell, of Carter's Creek, stands White Marsh. The grant for the land was made in the very early days of Gloucester's history, which began in the 1640's. White Marsh was the early seat of the Whitings, and remained in the possession of that family over a period of years. They built the main part of the present mansion about 1750. It was then a simple Georgian Colonial house, without wings or pillars.

The distinguished lawyer, Thomas Reade Rootes, owned White Marsh for a time. We find a note saying that Martha Jacquelin Cary gave a fortune to her nephew Thomas Rootes, Esq., of White Marsh. At Mr. Rootes' death his estate passed to his widow, who had been his second wife. She, too, had been married before; she left the estate to her children, who were Prossers, offspring of her first marriage.

One of the daughters, Evalina Mathilda Prosser, became the wife of John Tabb, son of Phillip Tabb, of Toddsbury. John bought out the interest of his sister-in-law in White Marsh, and he and Mathilda made it their home. At that time, after adding his wife's fortune to his own, John Tabb was said to have been the wealthiest man in Gloucester. There were then three thousand acres of land in the White Marsh Plantation, and from three hundred to five hundred slaves were employed to operate it. (1500 slaves rest in the slave graveyard, near the peach orchard.)

Mrs. Tabb did not wish to continue living in the country, but insisted upon moving to Norfolk or Williamsburg, in order to enjoy a gayer social

White Marsh showing front portico, magnificent box, and the largest ginkgo tree in America.

life. Mr. Tabb promised that if she would make herself content, and remain in the country, he would lay out for her the finest garden in Virginia.

It was then that the terraced gardens were built, and many rare and fine species of trees were planted in the park. It was also about this time that the house was remodeled, and the wings and pillared portico built.

Phillip, son of John and Evalina Mathilda Tabb, inherited White Marsh, while another son, John Prosser Tabb, received Elmington, over on the North River (see Part IV).

The Tabbs were related to the Lees and General Robert E. Lee was a visitor at White Marsh. He is reported to have said of White Marsh, "It is the most beautiful place I have ever seen." It was here, when he made his

38

White Marsh, from the playhouse portico.

last visit in 1868, that he gave a piece of heartfelt advice to Virginians, which has been much quoted in histories and Lee biographies. After dinner, while visiting with the Tabb family and guests in the parlor, one of the ladies present asked him,

"General Lee, what does the future hold for us poor Virginians now?"

"We must work for Virginia, and we must teach our children to love and cherish Virginia, and work for Virginia, that she may become great again."

General Lee occupied the northeast bedroom during that last visit to White Marsh, after the war. His son, Captain Robert Lee, was his roommate on this occasion.

39

Front view of White Marsh with its magnificent box.

In later years, Mr. H. M. Baruch, of New York, owned White Marsh, having bought it from W. J. Burlee, now of Tree Hill Farm, Henrico County. It was Mr. Baruch who planted the great profusion of boxwood which, in the years that have followed, have grown to such enormous proportions. He made his home here until 1942, when he sold to Horace Gray, Jr., of Waverly. The estate was later bought by Mr. and Mrs. C. H. Lawson, of Williamsburg.

There are various legends, or ghost stories told of White Marsh. It is said that Evalina Mathilda Tabb has been seen ascending the stairs in rustling silks. She goes immediately to the nursery and opens the drawers of the chests where the children's clothes were kept. She folds the tiny garments and replaces them. The tombstones in the family burying ground on the knoll back of the apple orchard, and overlooking the lower fields, attest that

The playhouse at White Marsh.

Evalina Mathilda lost two of her children in infancy.

Another story is that subsequent owners of the house on returning home late at night have found all lights on and have heard music, as of a dance or party coming from the house. As they alighted from carriages or cars, the lights went out, the music ceased, and the house again stood dark and silent.

Today there are a little over two thousand acres in the White Marsh Plantation, and it is now owned by Mr. and Mrs. William Ingles; Mr. Ingles is a tenth generation direct descendant of Lewis Burwell, the original grantee of 1642.

Almost every visitor who goes to White Marsh involuntarily agrees with General Lee that, "It is the most beautiful place I have ever seen." And why not? There are magnificent porticoes on both fronts. The children's play-house

41

(Above) The old ice house, in the garden at White Marsh.

ON FACING PAGE

(Above) White Marsh, showing the circle and end steps.

(Below) The gate into White Marsh.

42

Detail of stair-case at Airville.

has miniature reproductions of these pillars. There are more than a hundred varieties of fine old trees growing in a park of twenty acres, and along the borders of the mile-long avenue. Among these trees, there is the famous ginkgo, said to be the largest ginkgo in this country. Then there are pecan trees, which the Forest Service people declare are the largest they have ever seen. There are huge elms, enormous crepe myrtles, arbor vitae, boxwood, magnolia grandiflora, dogwood, cypress, holly, tulip poplar, Irish yew, Italian yew, shellbark, and several other varieties of hickory, several of oaks, maple, beech, horsechestnut, broadnut, butternut, Chinese chestnut, locust, black walnut, English walnut, filbert, cedar, Oregon spruce and many other varieties of trees.

The great size to which many of these trees have grown is attributed to the stratum of marl which underlies the land here. The green grass of the park, caressed by the shade of these trees, is of a quality of beauty that once seen enriches a lifetime.

At the back, from the terraces, a great vista of space is felt. The peach orchards; the apple orchards; the vast meadow, with its herd of beef cattle; and beyond the far trees, the Ware River; all these emphasize the extent, the largeness of White Marsh Plantation.

And the old house, with its big rooms and wide halls, shady and cool, rich in polished woodwork, sweet with the odor of many flowers, gives a feeling of home—a sense of fulfillment.

White Marsh has been dubbed "Queen of the Tidewater."

AIRVILLE

SITUATED on a high hill with a lovely view of well-cultivated fields running down to the Ware River, is Airville, home of the Dixons.

In some old notations of Gloucester we find that "John Dixon, Sr., of Airville, Gloucester Co., Va., only son (born 1778, died Sept. 5, 1830, buried at Mt. Pleasant, his father's home), married Sarah, daughter of Warner and Julia (Langborne) Throckmorton, and had issue:

"(a) John Dixon M.D., born 1812, died 24 June 1835, unmarried. (He was also buried at Mt. Pleasant.)

"(b) Harriet Peyton married Jacob Sheldon, and lived for many years in Williamsburg, Va."

Mrs. Page, of Shelly, tells of her Aunt Sarah, her mother's eldest sister, being married to Mr. Dixon of Airville. John, Sr., of Airville, was a son of The Rev. John Dixon, a colonial minister of nearby Mt. Pleasant, and his wife, Elizabeth Peyton, of Isleham. (Mt. Pleasant house is long since gone, but traces are discernible.)

Beautiful old Airville, now the home of Mr. and Mrs. Chandler Bates.

General Taliaferro, in writing of Gloucester, says that Airville is one of the old residences of the county, and goes on to add that "—all the old seats have their histories and traditions full of suggestions to romantic and imaginative minds."

In writing of the War of 1812, General Taliaferro says, "Our seabound situation rendered us liable to maritime incursion, and my father has often told me how as a boy he watched from the portico at Airville the manoeuvres of the British Fleet." (His father was Warner Throckmorton Taliaferro.)

Airville, overlooking the Ware and the Bay beyond, is a charming old frame structure, the oldest part of which was built by John Dixon in 1756.

46

There is a beautiful hall with unusual hanging stairway, and the house contains the original fine old woodwork.

In Airville, as in a few other old Virginia houses, is a secret chamber. This, of course, adds a note of mysterious glamour. The main building consists of a full basement, and two stories and a half, the third floor having dormer windows. Wings have been added. The architecture is in the Georgian influence. There is a small front porch with high steps.

From the Dixons the Airville estate passed to the possession of Major Thomas Smith and later to the Harwoods. The grounds, of natural beauty, are well kept, and the gardens have been restored.

It is now the home of Mr. and Mrs. Chandler Bates.

STARR LYNN

PART of the Airville estate was cut off some years ago and called Clermont. During this time, it was the home of Marius Jones and his wife, Mary Armi-

Starr Lynn, the house of General and Mrs. R. E. Starr, formerly part of Airville.

(Above) The old kitchen of Airville incorporated in this dwelling.

ON FACING PAGE

(Above) The living room at Starr Lynn, showing some of the priceless antiques the Starrs have collected and (below) the fine old oriental chest.

stead Cattlett. Later this property was sold to General and Mrs. R. E. Starr by Mr. Van Bibber Sanders, and a good deal of remodelling and restoring has been done and additions made. They have renamed the place Starr Lynn, incorporating the family name with Mrs. Starr's given name.

It is remarkable how General and Mrs. Starr have retained the beauty and tradition of the old place, yet have attained a thoroughly modern and comfortable home. The old quarters kitchen has become a modernized family kitchen—the only regrettable part being the removal of the huge old chimney.

Starr Lynn houses many priceless antiques. During General Starr's duty in the far East (or the far West!) Mrs. Starr made frequent trips into out-of-the-way places deep in the interior of the countries they visited, and from natives acquired valuable pieces of china, ivory, ebony, linens, and embroideries. Her furniture and rugs have been selected with infinite care, and the blending of decorations and furnishings have been effected with exquisite taste. The measure of age is not in American years, but Chinese and Japanese periods. One Chinese bowl Mrs. Starr has dates from a pre-Ming Period.

On the land belonging to Starr Lynn are the old slave graveyards of the Airville estate.

WILSON'S CREEK

GENERAL WILLIAM BOOTHE TALIAFERRO refers to Wilson's Creek (which has disappeared long ago) as a pre-Revolutionary home of Gloucester. In connection with the Throckmorton family we find that Thomas Throckmorton, of Wilson's Creek, son of Major Mordecai Throckmorton and grandson of Sir John Peyton, Baronet of Isleham, married Julia Lewis, daughter of Warner Lewis, of Warner Hall. The marriage took place April 29, 1815 at Severn House (*Richmond Enquirer*). He died without issue.

COLRAINE

ON Wilson's Creek, not far from the site of the old Wilson's Creek House, now stands Colraine, the modern home of Major and Mrs. W. Milner Gibson.

SHERWOOD

THIS attractive old place was a part of the Robins grant, and was for many years the home of the Seldens and Dimmocks, descendants of the Lewises of Warner Hall. It was originally called Shabby Hall.

With its Dutch type slate roof, its spacious piazzas, an excellent view

50

Colraine, the home of the Gibsons on Wilson's Creek. Not far from the old Wilson's Creek house site.

Sherwood, which faces the Ware. Notice the substantial chimneys!

52

of the river, in its setting of tree-studded grounds, this has been, and is still, an ideal country home.

Mrs. Robert Munford, a widow, went to live with her relatives at Belle Farm. Here she remained until her only surviving child grew up and was married to Mr. John Sinclair, of Shabby Hall. Mrs. Munford then went to live with her daughter, Margaret Ann, at Shabby Hall, later Sherwood. The Sinclairs left a number of descendants, who intermarried with the best Gloucester families.

Originally Sherwood was an L-shaped dwelling. When the house was remodeled, the original mantels and other beautifully carved woodwork were retained.

Sherwood is a large mansion, of Colonial style. Its third story dormers, and its tall chimneys can be seen from some distance. It was built in the eighteenth century.

Sherwood was purchased in 1830 by Mr. and Mrs. Robert Colgate Selden, and for many years remained in their family.

Mr. Selden's mother, Charlotte Colgate, of England, planned the garden. It was laid out in the shape of an H and was two hundred feet wide by four hundred feet long, flanked by crepe myrtles, and planted with many rare, beautiful and sweet flowers and shrubs. Mrs. Colgate copied an old English garden, and to this day many varieties of the plants she grew are still found at Sherwood. This garden was famed throughout the Tidewater and was resplendent with roses, lilacs, snowballs, pride of China, English bay, sweet bay, Cuban laurel, spirea, mock-orange, pomegranates, lilies, iris and Japonica.

The lawns were, and still are, dotted with large elms, magnolias, pecans, tulip poplars, and different varieties of maples.

The silver service of Abingdon was kept at Sherwood by Mrs. Selden.

Mrs. H. A. Williams, a grand-daughter of Mr. and Mrs. Robert Colgate Selden, and Mr. Williams were owners of Sherwood for many years, and they made their home here. It is now owned by Mr. and Mrs. James Ervin.

WHITE HALL

FRANCIS WILLIS, a native of Oxford, England, a member of the First Burgesses, member of the Council . . . died in London, leaving his Virginia property to his nephew, whose descendants long lived at White Hall.

Ann, the wife of Francis Willis, is buried under the chancel at Ware Church, and on her tombstone the arms of her own family are impaled on those of her husband. The old Willis home was known as Edge Ware. Just

White Hall, the home of Mr. and Mrs. George H. Cunningham.

54

when the name was changed is difficult to say. We do know there were several Francis Willises.

In 1751, Colonel Francis Willis (possibly the Third) gave "three pistoles" to Mr. Bacon's school in Talbot County, Maryland. Mrs. Willis gave a doubloon.

From *Education in Colonial Virginia* we learn that Francis Willis, of White Hall, in company with many other distinguished Virginians, attended the school in Gloucester County of Rev. William Yates, Minister of Abingdon Parish, in 1752. We think this must have been Francis IV.

We think it was this same Francis, (IV), who is spoken of as Francis Willis, the son of Francis Willis and Elizabeth Carter, and lived at White Hall. We have read a contract with "Nathan Jacobs, of the County of Frederick, distiller," which bargains for the making of good whiskey on the place at White Hall. This whiskey must be "merchantable; of sufficient proof." Mr. Willis allows Mr. Jacobs a holiday of twelve days, four times a year. Jacobs is to have "two able hands" to assist him, and Mr. Willis promises to lodge and board him.

This contract was dated September 19, 1793.

When this Francis Willis died, about December 4, 1797, he left a large fortune and nine children.

The *Virginia Gazette* says that he had warehouses and a bakery on Mobjack Bay. This must also have been the Francis Willis who rode horseback to Mount Vernon, to visit Washington for several days.

Miss Mary Willis, a descendant of Francis Willis, was married to Dr. Samuel Powell Byrd, who built the present White Hall in 1815. The estate descended to their son, Richard Corbin Byrd, who married a granddaughter of Chief Justice John Marshall.

White Hall has changed hands several times in the last fifty years. It was at one time owned by Harry E. R. Hall. His widow lived there for some years. She later became the Countess of Beatty, having married the Earl of Beatty, son of the hero of Jutland. At one time it was owned by Ernest C. Rollins, and later by John G. Hayes, Jr. Mr. Hayes sold the estate in 1947, to Mr. George H. Cunningham, a native of Culpeper, who came to White Hall from New Jersey.

Located on the Ware River near Zanoni Post Office, and about five miles from Gloucester Court House, White Hall is one of the very fine old Gloucester homes. It is a colonial type house with broad porches, many windows, huge chimneys, and large wings. The mansion stands three stories high, with the front facade having a large fanlight in the wide gable. The interior is beautifully decorated, and the mantels, staircases and window and door frames are in exquisite taste.

White Hall showing wing and chimney.

The estate consists of about two hundred and fifty acres. There is a huge, spreading lawn, and beautiful water front.

The crepe myrtles and boxwood here are magnificent. The old Willis graveyard is nearby.

GOSHEN

THE original seat of the Tompkies family (from which "Captain Sally," of Poplar Grove descended), Goshen on the Ware River, was built between 1750 and 1760.

The earliest unit of the house consisted of a central hall with a large square room on each side. Unusual features of this house were high mantels, and wainscote. There were also other details of the interior of an interesting and quaint character. About one hundred years after the house had been built, a section was added at the back, and still later, in 1926, a wing was added to each end.

The grounds take in a considerable acreage, with extensive gardens rebuilt around remaining crepe myrtles, and other shrubs.

Of the dependencies, one slave cabin and the original smokehouse have been preserved intact in the back.

In 1830 this property was brought by William Kennon Perrin, and for more than a hundred years remained in the Perrin family.

It is now owned by Mrs. George Mackubin, a descendant of the Perrins, and Mr. Mackubin.

A unique silver lard-oil lamp in the parlor belonged to Mrs. Mackubin's great-grandmother, of Alexandria.

The beautiful old silver service, inherited by the family, was originally owned by the mother of Matilda Prosser Tabb.

Family portraits by well-known artists adorn the walls, and the view across the lawns to the blue waters of the Ware enhance the beauty of a superb setting.

WAREHAM

THE original grant on which many generations of Cookes lived, was for 1174 acres in the Mobjack Bay region, to the first Mordecai Cooke, in 1650. The place was known as Wareham, and sometimes, also, as Warham. It was a very early seat of the Cooke family, on the Ware River, and in their house Governor Berkeley took refuge during Bacon's Rebellion. Berkeley occupied the old "Chamber," a room that he probably found convenient as a hiding place,

Land front of Goshen, the home of the Mackubins.

58

Another view of the land front of Goshen.

A substantial looking dependency at Goshen.

since there were some cubby-holes there in which he could take cover in case the rebels came looking for him.

We know there was a pre-Revolutionary mansion on the site, but we do not know whether it was the house in which Berkeley took refuge, or whether it was built later. In any event, there is no house now at Wareham.

Mordecai Cooke's son, John, married first Anne Todd, born 1682, died 1720, eldest daughter of Captain Thomas and Elizabeth Todd. Her tomb is at Wareham.

John's second wife was Mary Smith, born April 14, 1691, died March 15, 1724. Her tomb is also at Wareham. She was the eldest daughter of John and Elizabeth Smith.

60

A later Mordecai Cooke's tomb is at Wareham, as well. He was evidently the grandson of the first Mordecai, and was buried in 1751—aged forty-three. His wife, Elizabeth Whiting Cooke, born 1713, died 1762, is buried at Wareham, too.

The property now belongs to H. M. Mason and Brothers.

The dining room, in the oldest part of the house at Goshen.

Church Hill, the home of Mr. and Mrs. E. Wright Noble.

CHURCH HILL

THE original grant of 1174 acres of land to Mordecai Cooke was made in 1650. In 1658, a large brick house was built on the elevation just above the Ware River. This home was called Mordecai's Mount, and was one of the earlier "grand" homes of Gloucester County. The garden was laid out in four terraces, at the foot of which a long meadow extended to the Ware. The view from the windows and the terraces was said to have been very beautiful.

Mordecai Cooke was sheriff in Gloucester in 1698, and a member of the House of Burgesses in 1696. One of his daughters was Susan, who married Captain Henry Fitzhugh.

62

Another daughter, Frances, married Gabriel Throckmorton in 1690, and gave the land on which the present Ware Church was built soon after.

In the 1700's the main part of the house was burned, leaving a brick wing. To this a frame addition was made. Much later, the brick wing burned, after which the entire frame house was built on the old foundations, as an addition to the frame wing of earlier date.

The name, Mordecai's Mount, was changed pretty early to Church Hill.

The Cooke property passed in a direct line from the Cookes to their descendants, the Throckmortons. Then one of the two heiresses of the house of Throckmorton married Mr. William Taliaferro, and when she died, her sister and co-heiress married the widower. Thus the estate passed to the Taliaferros.

The Throckmortons had already been prominent in England before they migrated to America. They seem to have had some connection with royalty. They are spoken of during the reign of Henry the Eighth as "the ancient family of Throckmortons." And after their migration to Virginia, they became important both socially and politically in Gloucester. But today, although the name figures prominently elsewhere, it is no longer found in Gloucester. This, of course, is owing to the fact that the male members of the family moved away; but the women remained behind. Thus it is that those descendants of the Throckmortons still to be found in the county, no longer bear the Throckmorton name, because they trace their line back to female members of the clan.

From Mrs. Page's manuscripts we learn that her grandfather, Warner Throckmorton, married Mary Langborn (or Langbourne). Warner's brother, Mordecai, married Miss Peyton, of Isleham. Mrs. Page says her grandfather, Philip Throckmorton, married a Miss Smith.

A valuable genealogical brochure by Professor William Carter Stubbs, Ph. D., of Audubon Park, New Orleans, Louisiana, is very interesting. In this he traces the Cooke family from 1650, giving records of births, deaths, baptisms, college records, arms, etc. He includes an account of Mordecai Cooke and his descendants, also of other families, among them the Booths, Buckners, Baylors, Baytops, Burwells, Fauntleroys, Fitzhughs, Masons, Mallorys, Pauls, Thrustons, Taliaferros, Whitings and so forth.

Later, Dr. and Mrs. Stubbs enlarged this brochure into a book, (1923), called "Descendants of Mordecai Cooke."

Some of the distinguished descendants of the Cookes, Throckmortons and Taliaferros are General William Boothe Taliaferro, Major Thomas S. Taliaferro, Judge Beverley R. Wellford, Jr., Mrs. Nina Taliaferro Sanders, Judge Warner T. Jones.

The big chimney at Church Hill.

An interesting ghost story is told of Church Hill.

One of the owners of this estate, a Mr. Throckmorton, took his beautiful young daughter for a visit to London. There she met a handsome young English gentleman, with whom she fell deeply in love, and he with her. They both declared eternal faithfulness to each other, and arranged to complete plans for their marriage, by correspondence, after which he would follow her to Gloucester to claim her hand.

But the father would have none of it. He did not approve of the match, so all letters between the two were intercepted, and neither ever heard from the other.

The daughter fell ill and died. She was buried the afternoon after her death near sunset, in the family burying ground. That night the distraught father heard what he thought was a dog scratching at the door, but in his distress he paid no attention. The cook saw a pale face at the kitchen window, but in her fright, instead of informing the family, the terrified domestic fled to bed, not taking time to undress, but burying her face in the pillow and covering up her head.

The next morning, the manservant, whose duty it was to tidy up the front of the house, found the young girl's body on the front steps, covered with snow that had fallen during the night.

A manservant who had been unruly and rebellious, had been punished not long before the death of the daughter. To get his revenge, and because he knew she was buried with expensive jewelry, he had dug up the body, and cut off her finger to get her rings. The shock of this revived the girl from the coma which had been mistaken for death. She made her way to the house, but on account of her illness and inability to attract the attention of anyone to let her in, had died of exposure during the night. Ever after, the occupants of Church Hill on the first cold nights when snow is imminent, can hear the rustle of silken skirts passing from room to room, while the ghostly wearer is presumably making sure all the fires are replenished, so no one will suffer from the cold. There is a spot near the steps up to the house where the violets grow every year in lush profusion. They are finer here than those in any part of the grounds, for this spot was watered with the tears of the dying girl, on that tragic night so long ago.

Church Hill was for many years the lovely, well-kept home of Mr. and Mrs. E. Wright Noble. Among the improvements and alterations that were made is a huge chimney built of bricks brought from Rosewell.

The classic columns, the commodious proportions of the house, the excellent taste with which modern and comfortable furnishings are combined with fine antiques, all combine to enhance the atmosphere of this truly traditional Virginia country house.

This estate has recently been purchased by Mr. and Mrs. E. Stewart James, of Cappahosic House. They have decided to call their new home Church Hill Plantation.

PIG HILL

PIG HILL, now owned by the Kings, has a lovely location on the Ware River.

Originally a part of Glen Roy, it was formerly called Whiting's Mount, and was the seat of the Whiting family. After their day it passed through various hands. At one time it was owned by the Young Brothers, John G. Young, and W. Oscar Young, and by William C. King, Jr., of Pittsburgh.

It is a large, two-story house, of brick, painted white, and has a wing on either end with huge chimneys. The two-story columned portico has a second-floor balcony with Chinese chippendale railing. A small deck surmounting the roof has a similar railing. The large rooms are tastefully furnished, and the grounds, with big, old trees, shrubs, many flowers and lovely grass, are well-kept.

It was occupied by the Whiting family when the Scaife Whiting incident in Ware Church, about which the following poem was written, occurred. (Scaife's mother was Mrs. Mary Scaife Whiting.)

The Gloucester Herald
Gloucester C.H. Va.
Saturday, April 20, 1872
WM. B. Taliaferro and
Samuel D. Puller, Editors

(Ware Church)

A Tale of The Past.

To the Editor of the Herald: — Some two or three issues back you published in your valuable paper an original ballad, written in such pure and apposite English and combining so many of the excellences of the older and better ballad-writers; that, for myself and many others, I would beg the favor of its republication.

Respectfully,

'T'.

It was per chance, in times gone by,
 Some ninety years or more,
As strange a thing did hap I wot
 As e'er you heard before.

There lived a gay and dashing man,
 Scaife Whiting was his name;
In good old Gloucester, then as now,
 A place of noted fame.

To be afraid he knew not how,
 This was his boast and pride,
But surest things are not yet sure,
 And ill doth oft betide.

Now near him dwelt a jolly youth,
 Who was chock full of fun;
A brawny lad of sturdy mould,
 By name, Dick Singleton.

66

OLD VIRGINIA HOUSES

It so fell out one stormy night,
   In sunny, leafy June,
What time the storm king's gathering hosts,
   Did rout the pale-faced moon,

That these two gents benighted were,
   As home they hastened late.
Nor either knew the other near,
   Each cursed untoward fate.

Scaife rode a horse full mettlesome,
   Black as the wings of night,
And Dick bestrode one near as good,
   Its hue a creamy white.

Close by the road they both did wend
   A church was situate
"Old Ware," that by disuse had grown
   Ruined and desolate.

This was the only place where they,
   A refuge then might find,
To shelter from the drenching rain,
   And ward the furious wind.

Dick first arrived and doubtingly,
   Rode up the desert aisle,
Reined in his steed close to the wall
   And trembling paused a while.

While still his bosom agitates
   Twixt chilling fear and pride,
Scaife Whiting dashing through the door,
   In speedily doth ride.

Now thought Dick unto himself,
   It proven soon shall be
Whether yon daring Infidel
   Doth boast true bravery.

✿   ✿   ✿   ✿

And Scaife found as all alone,
   (At least he fancied so)
Within the church at that dread hour,
   His courage fleeting go.

Quoth he, " 'Tis true I am not afraid,
   And yet I feel not right,
Amongst the dead alone to be,
   At this deep hour of night."

As thus he speaks, the lightning gleams,
   And opposite he sees,
A sight that puts his hair on end,
   That makes his blood to freeze.

A ghostly steed of monster size,
   Doth bear a ghostly form,
Which grim, and stark, and full doth seem
   Lord of the awful storm.

✿   ✿   ✿   ✿

"What art thou? Speak," Scaife hoarsely
   shouts;
   A hollow groan replies.
"Fough!" now furiously he spurs
   In frantic haste he flies.

And follows swiftly on his track,
   With equal speed the ghost,
Cries Scaife, "Good steed, now do your best,
   Or I am surely lost!"

Full quickly fled the miles away,
   To him they seemed to stand,
Till to his breast's sincere relief,
   He sees his home at hand.

His courser's speed, no whit he slacks,
   But leaps unto the ground,
Nor till his door-knob firm he clasps,
   Doth dare to look around.

While there for an instant pausing,
   Contending with his fears,
He sees the pale steed pass his gate,
   A jeering laugh he hears.

"Now foul fiends sieze me!" loud he cries,
   "That I this night have run,
And shown a craven crest before the
   Eyes of Singleton!"

"Bear witness, Devils, on my oath,
    This hand his death shall seal.
Does he to any mortal dare
    This secret to reveal."

* * * *

The morrow's sun shone cheerily,
    A handsome banquet spread,
And laughing Dick to Whiting's comes
    Invited to break bread.

Scaife meets his guest most graciously,
    And ushers in his door;
"A glorious day we will have," quoth he,
    And deep libations pour."

* * * *

Dinner finished, the board is cleared,
    The servants now retire,
First on the table placing wine
    To light convivial fire.

"Ere you to jovial duties turn,
    I, your attention crave,
A moment, will not long delay
    Bacchanalian rites," quoth Scaife.

So speaking, to the door he goes
    And locks and bars it fast
Then from his breast a pistol draws,
    With ire his face o'er cast.

Reseats himself, "and thus bold Dick
    The truth you fain must tell,
If that to any you have spoke
    Of what last night befell."

"I have not breathed a syllable,"
    Instanter answered Dick,
"But what the thunder ails you, man?
    What means this savage trick?"

"You hold!" said Scaife "a secret far
    To me, than life more dear;
In that last night you saw me yield
    To coward dastard fear.

"And if your life you would preserve,
    Nor anxious are to die;
This secret promise still to keep
    And guard most sacredly."

* * * *

"You must confirm it with an oath,
    And swear as I dictate,
That never while I live, a word
    Of this you will relate."

Dick swore and faithfully he kept
    The oath that night he spoke,
Long years had passed and Scaife was dead,
    E're he his silence broke.

The above was written by Judge Fielding Lewis Taylor, of Belle Farm, Gloucester, Va.

N. T. S.

At the time of the above incident, Scaife Whiting lived at Pig Hill near the head of Ware River, and Dick Singleton lived at Bloomsbury on North River.

GLEN ROY

ON a peninsula in the Ware River, is the oldest church site in Gloucester. It is here that Glen Roy was built. On one side is what is known as Churchfield, on the other is Glebefield. There are still tombs in Churchfield.

Pig Hill, formerly called Whiting's Mount, now belongs to the Kings.

Here the Reverend Armistead Smith, a descendant of the old Smith family, of Gloucester, and of the Honorable John Armistead, of Hesse, member of the Colonial Council, brought home his bride, the former Martha Tabb, of Seaford in Mathews County. He served as Rector of two colonial churches, Abingdon and Ware.

The house in which they lived was burned, and their son, Mr. William Patterson Smith, built the mansion known now as Glen Roy. He married the beautiful Miss Marian Seddon, of Fredericksburg, and together for many years they kept up the traditions of Glen Roy.

This was also the home of the Smiths, Tylers and Seawells, who intermarried.

A later owner was Mr. W. R. Jaeger, who left the estate to John G. Young and his brother, W. Oscar Young.

Although Scaife Whiting's home was Pig Hill (or Whiting's Mount as it was then called), we find a notation which says Colonel Scaife Whiting, of Glen Roy, was Justice in 1794; died in 1821. Pig Hill was originally a part of Glen Roy, and of course it is probable that Colonel Whiting, through inheritance or purchase, acquired Glen Roy and spent his later life there.

It is now the home of Dr. Edwin T. Wellford, and his family. They trace back their line to Mrs. Armistead Smith, wife of the original owner.

This handsome Georgian type home has first floor ceilings sixteen feet high, and second floor ceilings fourteen feet high. It has dormer windows, and stands three stories high. The wide porches, broad lawns, enormous trees and lovely view make Glen Roy a choice place to live.

The present house was built late in the eighteenth century.

LOWLAND COTTAGE

DURING the War of 1812 we find reference, in the writings of General William B. Taliaferro, to Captain Richard Jones, of Lowland Cottage, as being among those who commanded the troops defending our shores. This Captain Jones married Martha, daughter of Warner Throckmorton and Julia Langborne. (Mrs. Page's manuscript; also *Richmond Standard*.)

The Cottage, with its beautiful old trees and wide lawns, is one of the oldest homes in Gloucester. It is an L-shaped house, of early Colonial style. Built about 1690, this was an early seat of the families of Warner, Throckmorton, Jones, Taliaferro, and is now the home of Major and Mrs. Jeffery Montague.

The chimneys and the planting around The Cottage give evidence of its age. With two end chimneys and one middle chimney and with gable windows and gambrel-roof, the structure seems of simple plan, but the rooms

Glen Roy, the home of Dr. E. T. Wellford.

A dependency at Glen Roy.

72

are large and homey. The Cottage is a pleasant place to live in, and the fruit trees and flowing shrubs around it enhance the impression of friendly live-ableness.

HOCKLEY

ADJACENT to The Cottage is Hockley, a spacious, colonial house, which was long the home of the Taliaferros. In olden times the place was called Cowslip Green, also Erin. Hockley has attractive grounds, with old plantings.

It now belongs to Marian Canfield and Annie Hayes O'Neil.

LEVEL GREEN

LEVEL GREEN was the old home of the Robins family, but has been out of the family now for many years. It was built early in the 18th century. Around the house are huge, beautiful old trees, and velvety lawn dotted with box and other shrubs. Built of brick, with gable windows and huge chimneys, the effect is quaint and lovely.

It is here that Henry Clay once landed during a political campaign in this part of the country.

Level Green is now owned by William T. Kilborn.

BAIAE

BAIAE, a small place on the Ware, was formerly owned by John Taliaferro, who probably was the builder. It was later owned by a Mr. Eels. During the Civil War, Baiae became a hospital. After living at Elmington a few years, Colonel Munford, who married a Miss Ellis, and who was author of *The Two Parsons*, bought Baiae, and made it the family home for some years. (Miss Etta Munford, the daughter of Colonel Munford, now lives in Richmond.) Baiae was next owned by Mr. Fox, to whom it was sold by Colonel Munford.

After Mr. Fox, Mr. Augustus Drury, of Richmond, lived at Baiae for some years. It has undergone many alterations, and has been modernized.

The house and the great oaks at Level Green. Notice the river in the background.

76

PART FOUR
ON THE NORTH RIVER

DITCHLEY

IN writing of the social life of Gloucester in the 1890's, Mrs. Sally Nelson Robins, speaking of beaux, says: "Young men are delightful adjuncts, but by no means the perfunctory articles they have gotten to be in 1893." She goes on to tell of a friend who came to spend the day and stayed forty-five years. Social life in Gloucester, no matter of what period, has always, it may truly be said, centered around North River—possibly because the estates there could be reached so conveniently by water. And that is why, no doubt, this section has been called the Venice of America.

The first old house on the left, as one sails into the North from the Mobjack Bay, is Ditchley. It was originally the home of the Singletons, and was called Bloomsbury. In 1862 this place was bought by Professor Edwin Taliaferro, of Belleville. He restored and remodeled the house, and beautified the grounds, calling it Miramer, because of the beautiful and clear reflection it made in the blue water. However, the house was burned down before he moved in.

When the property was acquired in 1863 by Dr. John Prosser Tabb, he built a home on the site of the earlier dwelling, naming the place Ditchley, for Ditchley in England. This was in honor of his wife, who was related to the Lee family, of English Ditchley.

In 1898, Ditchley was purchased by Mr. and Mrs. William Ashby Jones, of Richmond. The house has been remodeled and is now owned by Mr. and Mrs. William Ashby Jones III.

77

BELLEVILLE

BELLEVILLE, on one of the most beautiful sites on the south side of the North River, was built on the land acquired by John Boswell and John Booth, in a grant from the crown in the seventeenth century. This grant adjoined other land on the North River, already owned by Booth. These two gentlemen were wholesale tobacco buyers, who did an export business between Gloucester and London. Their office, a brick building with a huge fireplace, is still standing. It is close by the Belleville mansion, and for years was used as a kitchen.

The original mansion was an H-shaped brick building, which faced the river. It was built about 1658. When it burned some years later, only a five-room brick wing remained. A substantial frame building was added to this. The parlor, with a large fireplace to the north, had on each side a deep recess, beautifully arched, in which was a window of tiny panes; there was a wide window-seat, on which many a child curled up and read the Standard Works. This room and the adjoining dining room were paneled from ceiling to floor. Both rooms had the deep windows and high mantels.

In 1705 Thomas Booth, a descendant of John, acquired the entire property by indenture. It was passed by inheritance to Frances Amanda Todd Booth and her husband, Warner Throckmorton Taliaferro, and from them to their son, William Booth Taliaferro.

During the lifetime of Mr. Warner Taliaferro, Belleville reached a high peak of production and development. There were large barns, a harness shop, saw-pit, shoe-shop, weaving-house, blacksmith shop and carpenter shop, besides servants' quarters, stables and carriage houses.

Practically everything used on the plantation was made there; even the boats used on the river were constructed of lumber cut from local trees; the nails used were made in the blacksmith shop.

Mr. Taliaferro's second marriage was to Miss Leah Seddon, of Fredericksburg. It was she who laid out a new garden around what was left of the box walk and the enormous crepe myrtles of the old garden. She introduced every variety of flower and shrub adaptable to the climate. With its natural, parklike setting, and lovely view of the river, Belleville became one of the show places of the area.

Some years after the death of General William Booth Taliaferro, his son George Booth Taliaferro sold the place to Mr. A. A. Blow. Thus Belleville passed from the family of Booths and their descendants, the Taliaferros, after it had been in their possession for two hundred and fifty years.

Mr. Blow built a pillared portico, and made other changes in the house.

Dr. and Mrs. H. E. Thomas purchased Belleville early in 1930 and for

The old part of the house at Belleville, originally the home of the Booths.

An avenue at Belleville.

ON FACING PAGE

(Above) Chimneys, dormers and roses at Belleville, the boyhood home of General William Booth Taliaferro. (Below) A massive chimney at Belleville.

80

The Morck's living room at Belleville, from which an excellent view of the river can be had.

a number of years lived there, but they sold it a few years ago to Mr. and Mrs. Wesley C. Morck, who now make it their home. Its magnificent box and beautiful garden draw visitors from all parts of the country.

In the cemetery, Booth tombs, with arms, may still be seen.

WARRINGTON

NEAR Belleville is Warrington, the large comfortable modern home of General William Booth Taliaferro's daughter, Mrs. H. O. Sanders. This place has the advantage of the same magnificent view of the river as Belleville, and now Warrington is as popular a center for social gatherings of the community as Belleville was in days of yore.

82

Dunham Massie, originally General William Booth Taliaferro's
home. Now the home of the Worths.

DUNHAM MASSIE

WARNER THROCKMORTON TALIAFERRO, of Church Hill, married
Frances Amanda Todd Booth, and went to live at Belleville, the Booth home.
When their son (and only child), William Booth Taliaferro, was married, his
father built a beautiful home for him on adjoining land near the river. It was
a two-story house with steep roof, and pointed gables. There were big center chimneys and a large front porch. It had an English look. It was finished
in 1847 while the son was serving in the Mexican War. This place was named

83

Burgh Westra, the home of the Marshalls.

Dunham Massie, in honor of the ancestral Booth home, near Chester, in England—which is still occupied by Booth descendants.

William Booth Taliaferro became a Major General in the Confederate Army, and was an important citizen for many years, serving as Judge of Gloucester County.

At Dunham Massie, on its spacious front porch with an extensive view of North River, were entertained a charming and delightful society of churchmen, statesmen, and gracious ladies of an older regime; but as long as General Taliaferro lived, each guest, so it was said, had to walk under a Confederate flag as he entered the door.

The family sold the place in 1939 to Mr. and Mrs. A. Carlton McKenney, of Richmond, and it is now owned by Mr. and Mrs. Mathew Fontaine Maury Werth.

BURGH WESTRA

NEXT to Elmington, on the North River, the attractive little home known as Burgh Westra was built for Dr. Philip Alexander Taliaferro, by his father, Warner Throckmorton Taliaferro, about 1847. For many years Dr. Taliaferro lived here, where much entertaining was done. After the Doctor's death the place passed first to his wife, then to his sister, and finally to his favorite great niece, Susan Seddon Taliaferro Wellford Marshall (Mrs. Thomas R. Marshall, of Richmond). Built of brick, this substantial building has weathered beautifully the passing of the years. There are many nice shrubs and trees, also flowers, and a lovely river view. Furnished with antiques and reproductions, Burgh Westra is much enjoyed as a summer home by Mrs. Marshall, her children and grandchildren.

ELMINGTON

IN Gloucester, on the North River, approached from the highway by a long straight drive bordered with cedars, is Elmington. Located on a knoll, surrounded by a beautiful lawn, which sweeps out to the river beyond, this century-old mansion of white-washed brick, is one of the most impressive homes in the Tidewater. The white-wash is a kind of plaster treatment that makes the walls look like alabaster. The grounds are dotted with huge magnolias, crepe myrtles, box-woods, cedars and enormous elms.

In November, 1642, a patent to land on which Elmington stands was given to Edmund Dawber, of London. His wife's name was Margaret; she was a daughter of Sir Thomas Gates, a very early Colonial Governor of Virginia. This patent was renewed, or "cleared," seven years later, March 18, 1649, as was customary, to prove that the claim was in good faith, the land "seated," settled, and cultivated. Included in the patent was a tract of 2400 acres on the North River, and other land elsewhere.

Meanwhile, the massacre of 1644 and other circumstances prevented the issuance of further patents in Gloucester for some time.

However, on March 19th, 1652, a patent was issued for this same land, to William Deynes. This patent declared, after quoting dates of the Dawber patent, and renewal, that "—since deserted and granted by order of the Assembly—unto sd William Deines—"

Deynes had to face some disturbing "claymes" to his grant, as is evidenced by a rather formidable document of 1660 in the form of a deed from Dawber's heirs to Richard Young and John Prise, executed in London, and recorded in York County. Apparently Deynes became discouraged and relinquished his claim to at least a part of the North River property.

85

Elmington, the home of Mr. and Mrs. W. S. Rhoads, Jr.

Richard Young was issued a patent for the Elmington tract by Governor Berkeley in 1665. Before his death the same year, Young willed the land to his son, Richard, Jr., saying, "My son Richard to take in satisfaction of his share my plantation which I hold jointly with Dorcas Price, widow, lying at Mobjack Bay, near York River in Virginia."

Richard Young, Jr., was frequently in court about various matters, once in connection with a wager with Mr. Humphrey Gwynn about a servant maid.

There was also, on another occasion, a suit between Mr. Young and Mr. Henry Whiting, over a tobacco house on a certain parcel of land.

Later; Young petitioned the Governor and the Council to have Major John Lewis appointed "to lay out" the borders of his land according to his "ancient knowne bounds." Richard Young, Jr., left the Elmington estate to

The front entrance to Elmington.

his son, but under date of December 22, 1682, a patent for 2673 acres was made to Mr. John Buckner and Major Henry Whiting. This ended a period of twenty-seven years during which the Youngs had resided on the tract.

On a Quit Rent Roll, in Ware Parish, Gloucester, in 1704-5, from Governor Nicholson to England, we find the following acreage; John Buckner, 900 acres; Henry Whiting, 800 acres; Madm. Whiting, 950 acres; Thomas Todd, 884 acres. The conclusion is reached that the land had been divided; that John Buckner was John Buckner, Junior; that Henry Whiting was Henry Whiting, Junior; and that Madm. Whiting was Henry Whiting, Sr.'s, widow. It was during the Whiting ownership that the name Elmington was bestowed on the estate.

Henry Whiting, Jr., married Ann, daughter of Peter Beverley. Their children were: Elizabeth, who married John Clayton, the famous botanist,

87

and lived at Windsor; Catherine, who married John Washington, of Highgate, and became the great-aunt of General George Washington; and Beverley, their son, who inherited Elmington. He married Mary Scaife. He was educated at Oxford, in 1740 was a member of the House of Burgesses, and died in 1755.

Beverley's son, Peter Beverley Whiting, succeeded his father as owner of Elmington. He was educated at William and Mary College, became a vestryman of Ware Parish, and Sheriff of Gloucester. He married Elizabeth, daughter of Lewis Burwell, of Carter's Creek.

Peter Beverley Whiting II married Elizabeth Peyton, who was probably the granddaughter of Sir John Peyton, of Isleham. He evidently did not live long, for during the Revolution, when bad days had come to Elmington, the place is referred to as "Mrs. Whiting's." Mr. Philip Taliaferro reported to General Washington on October 3, 1781, "A party of the Enemy are now at Mrs. Whiting's and have sent out to collect the cattle and sheep adjacent there being no one to stop them."

In July of 1788 "a dreadful storm and highest tide ever known" swept away crops and livestock, thus removing subsistence for the next year. Houses were blown down, and other damage done.

As though this were not enough, in 1790 Mrs. Whiting was called on to settle her late husband's obligations as security for the deputies of Sir John Peyton, when sheriff in 1782-3, of Gloucester County. The Court order said in part: "It shall be lawful for Elizabeth Whiting, Adms. of Peter Beverley Whiting, decd. . . . to deliver and put in the hands of the afore named commissioners . . . all and every slave and Slaves, which now remain in their respective possessions . . . to be sold for satisfying the balance due. . . ."

Peter Beverley III is mentioned in 1800 as being a vestryman of Ware Parish. Old Mrs. Whiting died December 6, 1803. In 1804, after a hundred and twenty years of Whiting ownership, Elmington was sold by Peter Beverley Whiting III, now of Berryville, to Mr. Benjamin Dabney, a prominent lawyer of King and Queen County.

Mr. Dabney died in 1806, in the second year of his residence at Elmington. When some years later his widow arranged for a second marriage, their son, Thomas Smith Gregory Dabney was called to take over possession of Elmington. The house at this time was "of red brick, quaint and oldfashioned," and probably Colonial in style, with some Georgian influences. It was said to have been quite close to the river, and must, even in those days, have been imposing, for when Mr. Thomas Dabney brought home his beautiful bride, the former Sophia Hill, aged sixteen, she was so overcome with awe at the grandeur and magnificence of the place, and the many servants, that she did not dare to take over her housekeeping responsibilities for a matter

88

Elmington river front, showing edge of big magnolia.

of two years. She was Mr. Dabney's second wife. In 1820 he had married Mary, daughter of Chancellor Samuel Tyler. She died three years later. Then, after three years had elapsed, the handsome young widower courted and married the aforesaid lovely Sophia. That was in 1826.

For nine years this young couple lived at Elmington, entertaining hospitably many distinguished guests. In those days, a signal from post or tree meant an invitation to all the families up and down the river, to come for some gay festivity. John Tyler, later President of the United States, was a frequent guest at Elmington. In 1835 the Dabneys moved to Mississippi, and a few years later John Tabb, of White Marsh, bought Elmington for his son John Prosser Tabb, who married Miss Rebecca Lloyd, of Alexandria.

It was in 1848 that the present house was built. The beautiful old place was a wedding gift to Rebecca, who was as lovely a bride as Sophia Hill

Great hall at Elmington, showing circular stairs, grandfather's clock and historic scenes on walls.

had been, and her husband, John Prosser Tabb. There was a fine Hubard portrait of Rebecca, hanging in the home. The couple apparently lived in great style. It is said that Rebecca's cupboard was filled with dishes of gold and silver.

The hospitality and gracious living at Elmington were interrupted by the coming of the Civil War. Dr. John Prosser Tabb and his wife sold Elmington to Mr. James M. Talbott, of Richmond, and it was paid for with Confederate money.

Mr. Talbott leased the estate soon after, for a term of three years, to Colonel George Wythe Munford, who wrote *The Two Parsons* while resident there. The Munfords, however, only stayed at Elmington about two years.

The next owner of Elmington was Mr. Duncan; then just before the end of the century, Mr. Thomas Dixon, the famous novelist, bought and remodeled the house, renaming it Dixondale. It was he who built the pillared portico. While Mr. Dixon was resident here, he wrote some of his best books.

It seems that this spacious mansion on the river was destined to figure further in our literature, for more recently, Mr. Virginius Dabney has made it the scene of *Don Miff,* which was a best seller of the year in which it was published.

Mr. Dixon sold to Mr. Walkup, and he to Mr. Dimmock. The Dimmock possession lasted from 1908 to 1940, when Mrs. Walcott, the former Mrs. Dimmock, sold to Mr. Richard Smith, who in 1941 sold to Mr. and Mrs. Webster S. Rhoads, Jr., the present owners. So reads the list of owners of Elmington, for a period of three hundred and seven years.

Today, Elmington has a pillared portico on each front, and its appearance when approached by water or land, is most imposing. The great hall

Dining room at Elmington.

Sun room at Elmington.

ON FACING PAGE

(Above) Living room at Elmington.

(Below) Drawing room at Elmington.

reminds one of the great hall at Monticello. The scenic wall panels here depict episodes in American history. The spiral staircase ascends to the third floor, where there is an observatory with a unique arrangement of windows. A chandelier is suspended from the ceiling of the third floor, dropping down through the stair well, to light the great hall on the first floor.

The rooms are large, and have beautiful windows, mantels and chandeliers. They are furnished in exquisite taste, both in color combination and suitability of furnishing. The sheen of antique furniture, the gleam of old silver, and flowers everywhere, combine to create an atmosphere of charm and beauty as glamorous as what we like to think was characteristic of the fabled days of old.

EXCHANGE

THE Dr. Dabney home on the North River just above Elmington, is called The Exchange. It has been the home of the Dabneys for several generations. The Misses Dabney, whose mother was a Miss Tabb, of Toddsbury, long dispensed hospitality at the Exchange.

Tombs there show that this estate must previously have been the Anderson home.

One tomb reads:

> Mary Anderson
> born 27 August 1749
> died 12 June 1820

Another:

> Mathew Anderson, Esq.,
> born 6 December 1743
> died 24 December 1806

A third tomb has this inscription:

> George Dabney Anderson
> son of Mathew and Mary
> born October 8, 1760
> died Sept. 9, 1771
> (followed by consoling poetic
> quotation typical of the period).

Exchange, the home of the Dabneys.

Exchange was lent distinction by the famous artist, Hubard, well known in Gloucester County. The portraits he did which hung at the Exchange were: one of Thomas Todd Tabb; one of his wife, Elizabeth Foreman; one of Martha Tompkins, who married Dr. Henry Wythe Tabb, of Auburn, and left four daughters and one son; and one of Dr. James Dabney. Hubard also did a portrait of Elizabeth Perrin Page Michie, but if this was ever hung at Exchange, it was removed at an early date.

A unique feature of Exchange is the charming living quarters, both comfortable and modern, into which the picturesque old ice-house has been converted.

95

The Exchange was presumably built in the late eighteenth century, and is Georgian style, of frame construction. There is a front porch. Large chimneys are at the ends, and there is one wing.

HAIL WESTERN

JOHN THROCKMORTON married Miss Washington and lived on the Northern Neck, but returned to Gloucester after her death. There were several children by this marriage. After making financial arrangements for the care of these children, he married a Miss Cooke, of Gloucester, and went to England to receive an inheritance which had been willed to him there. When he returned to Gloucester he built a home and called it Hail Western (or Weston) in honor of an old home of the Throckmortons in England.

There was one child of this second marriage, a daughter, Eliza, whom Mrs. Page calls "Cousin Eliza Jones."

Hail Western was burned many years ago, but the outbuildings are still standing. They are frame, and have been converted into modern homes. It is away from the rivers but not far from the Ware.

TODDSBURY

ON the North River, in Gloucester, with its lawns sweeping right down to the water's edge, stands Toddsbury, a silent witness to almost all of Gloucester County's past, for it was in 1658 that the oldest part of the house was built. Thomas Todd, the emigrant, was the builder, and the place remained in the possession of his direct descendants for over two hundred years.

For four generations the owners were Todds; then Phillip Tabb, the son of Lucy Todd and Edward Tabb, married his cousin, Mary Mason Wythe, a daughter of Elizabeth Todd, and inherited Toddsbury from their uncle, Christopher Todd. Both these young people were direct descendants of Thomas Todd, the founder. Their descendants were owners for many years. Various additions and improvements were made to the house up until 1784.

The house is in purest Dutch Colonial style, with gambrel roof and shallow dormer windows. The body is of stucco over brick.

The central hall may be entered from the porch on the river front, or from the triangular terrace, which is now enclosed, on the garden front. Entrance may also be made from this terrace to the hall of the old wing, which stands at right angles to the larger part of the building. (This enclosed terrace is said to have previously been a "mud room," where shoes were scraped, boots removed, etc.)

Deeply recessed windows, beautiful old paneling, staircases and mantels

96

*Toddsbury, home of Mr. and Mrs. Gordon Bolitho. Notice garden wall
in background, also river and big trees.*

contribute to the beauty of the interior. The woodwork has the coveted patina
that comes from daily polishing, and daily use, throughout the centuries.

Toddsbury is homelike, and gives the impression of having been comfortably lived in for many generations. This is not surprising, since it has
been pretty continuously occupied ever since it was built. There have been
few days during the old mansion's three hundred year life-span that have
not seen smoke curling up out of at least one of the great chimneys, and on
chilly days at twilight, a wood fire in one of the six fireplaces of the house
has always brightened at least one room with its cheerful glow.

There must have been gay parties here; cheerful teas; hunt breakfasts;
romantic courtships. This old house must have been the scene of many wed-
dings, christenings, births, deaths and funerals. The family burying ground
is to the east of the house.

Toddsbury river front showing "porch" chamber.

The Motts came after the Tabbs, and they stayed over fifty years.

Now Mr. and Mrs. Gordon Bolitho are the owners. She is a direct descendant of the original builder of the house.

One of the unusual features of Toddsbury is the enclosed chamber above the porch, the "morning room," facing the river.

Some of the dependencies are still standing.

There was originally a beautiful formal garden, enclosed by a brick wall. Mr. and Mrs. Bolitho have restored both.

The large spacious lawns which are bordered by the river on three sides, are studded with ancient oak, elm and pecan trees.

Toddsbury is sometimes referred to as "The Jewel of the Tidewater."

In a letter from Mr. Gordon Bolitho, he says in part:

"Over the almost three hundred years since the original house was built, the place has apparently sunk about two feet. It is estimated that all of Tidewater is sinking one foot per century. However, in our cellar we have found the remains of a Dutch Oven, partially sunken now, with a flu running up what was originally the outside wall, now the wall of the library. In restoring the house we discovered numerous 'dated' bricks. The present sitting-room wing was added in 1722 and obviously the panelling taken out of part of the library for the walls of the sitting-room. The wall between library and hall is an ordinary partition which must have been put in when the sitting-room was added. The panelling of the library and sitting-room are identical but the woodwork in the hall is of a much later period. The present dining-room was added to in 1784 with bricks dated and initialed 'P.T.' (Philip Tabb?) and 'R.D.L.' "

The following Todd Genealogy, compiled from papers of Selina L. Hopkins, of Waverley, Gloucester County, and from family records lent us by Mrs. Nina Taliaferro Sanders, would be of great interest to descendants of the Todd family, the Tabb family, the Booths and Armisteads.

1. Geoffry Todd, sometimes spelled Tood, Toode, Todde, was of Hanghton-le-Sherne, a parish about five miles from Denton County, Durham, England. Buried February 22, 1637/8.

        Married Margaret.
        Their son—

2. Captain Thomas Todd, came from Denton, England to Toddsbury, Ware Parish, North River, Gloucester County, Virginia, and went later to Todd's Neck, North Parish, Patapsco River, Baltimore County, Maryland, where he settled in 1664. His will, and those of his son, Thomas Todd II, and his grandson, Thomas, are on record in the Courthouse of Baltimore County. He died at sea, 1676. Was baptised, September 12, 1619. Married Anne Gorsuch, issue, nine children of which the eldest:

3. Thomas Todd II, or Junior, was born at Toddsbury 1660. Justice of the Peace for Gloucester County from 1698 to 1702. Died January 16, 1724/5. Buried at Toddsbury. His will dated January 1714-15 on file in Baltimore County, Maryland, devises his "Lands in the neck where I now live" to his sons, Thomas and Robert, and if they have no heirs, to his brothers, William or Philip or Christopher on condition that whoever gets them shall live on them. Showan Hunting Grounds in draught of Gunpowder River to his son Robert. "All lands of mine in Virginia to be sold, except that on which I lived, and proceeds to be divided between my wife and children." He married Elizabeth Bernard, daughter of Colonel William Bernard and Lucy Higginson.

Issue of Thomas Todd II. Thomas Bernard, moved to his grandfather's

99

The hall at Toddsbury, showing antique chest with paintings of
Maria Louisa, fourteenth child of James II.

estate in Todd's Neck, Maryland. Robert, who inherited Showan Hunting Grounds, Maryland. William. Anne, who married Thomas Cooke, of Wareham, Gloucester County, Virginia. Philip, Sheriff of Gloucester in 1730. Frances. Frances 2nd. Elizabeth. Christopher.

4. Christopher (ninth child of Thomas Todd II and Elizabeth Bernard). Born at Toddsbury, April 2, 1690, and died at Toddsbury, his home, March 26, 1743. Buried at Toddsbury. Married in 1738, Elizabeth Mason (1701-1764), daughter of Lemuel Mason.

Issue of Christopher Todd. Lucy, born 1721, died 1794. Married in 1749, Edward Tabb, son of John and Martha Hand Tabb; Edward Tabb was born 1719; died 1782. They lived in Cumberland County for a time and came from there to live with her brother, Thomas Todd, after the death of their mother, at Toddsbury. When Thomas Todd died, he left Toddsbury to his sister, Lucy, and thus Toddsbury came into the Tabb family.

5. Elizabeth (daughter of Christopher Todd and Elizabeth Mason), born

100

Detail of alcove and paneling at Toddsbury.

101

The Library at Toddsbury.

ON FACING PAGE

(Above) The living room at Toddsbury (and below) the dining room.

Master bedroom at Toddsbury. Notice paneling and deep windows.

1723; died 1785. Married first, Nathaniel Wythe of Warwick County, and had a daughter, Mary Mason. Elizabeth married, second, Mordecai Booth, of Belle Ville, Gloucester County.

6. Mary Mason Wythe (daughter of Elizabeth Todd and Nathaniel Wythe) married, first, her step-brother, George Booth, of Belle Ville, son of Mordecai Booth and his first wife, Joyce Armistead of Hesse, Mathews County. Mary Mason Wythe married, second, Philip Tabb of Toddsbury, (her first cousin), son of Thomas T. Tabb.

Issue of Mary Mason Wythe and Philip Tabb: John, of White Marsh; Henry Wythe, of Auburn; Philip Edward, of Waverley; Thomas Todd, of Toddsbury.

Guest room at Toddsbury.

105

Newstead, home of the Holcombes, formerly a Tabb home.

NEWSTEAD

ON the North River, near Toddsbury, of which it was originally a part, stands Newstead. This, too, was a Tabb home. Built near the middle of the 19th century by John H. Tabb, it remained in the Tabb family for almost a century. It now belongs to Colonel and Mrs. John Lee Holcombe.

The house, of red brick with many gables and chimneys, and several porches, stands in a grove of large trees. A huge wing runs back at right angles to the main building. The style is Early American. There is a large area of lawn, and extensive gardens are being restored.

The father of the present owner lived for years in China, and Colonel Holcombe, himself, has visited there several times, so it is not surprising that the Holcombes have a magnificent collection of Chinese curios. There are in this collection many valuable pieces of carved ivory, as well as a handsome Chinese bowl, said to be 1500 years old. The Holcombes also have at New-stead a very extensive library and a large collection of 19th century paintings,

106

among which is a Rembrandt Peale, a Sully, a Trumbull, a Hubard, and the famous Charles II, by Edward Wissing.

WAVERLEY

ABOVE Newstead, on the North River, was built, about one hundred fifty years ago, the commodious mansion known as Waverley. It was built by Captain Philip Tabb, of Toddsbury, for his son, Philip Edward, at about the time he built Auburn for another son, Dr. Harry Tabb. Waverley is a Colonial type house in Georgian influence.

Captain Tabb, the builder of Waverley, distinguished himself in the War of 1812 by running the Blockade. He used his own men and his own ships in these adventurous expeditions. Captain Tabb left many descendants who became prominent, among them the late John Lightfoot, Esq., Mrs. Brown, who was a Miss Lightfoot, Judge Crump Tucker, and the late Dr. Beverley Randolph Tucker.

Philip Edward Tabb, Captain Tabb's son, for whom Waverley was built, married Miss Mary Almond of Norfolk. Their daughter became the wife of Judge William W. Crump, of Richmond, and left many descendants in Richmond.

Waverley, a beautiful home of brick construction, was enhanced by a marble porch and steps. This spacious mansion had a wide hall with very handsome curved stairway. There were two large rooms at the back and one to the right of the hall.

Tombs at Waverley indicate that there was a previous house on this site.

One of the tombstones reads:

> In Memory of Doctor
> Richard Edwards
> Who departed
> This Life the 8
> Day of March in
> The Year 1721
> Having had two
> Wives and at the
> Time of his Death
> Nine Children
> Living
> (Skull and crossbones)

Midlothian, home of the Moormans.

Another of the tombs is not entirely decipherable, but we learn that an earlier Richard Edwards died in March 1707.

Waverley was sold first to Dr. Jones, later to Mr. Hopkins, a nephew of Johns Hopkins of Baltimore.

Mrs. Snowden Hopkins, now of River's Edge, Gloucester County, was residing at Waverley at the time it was burned—some years ago. Mrs. R. M. Janney, of Roaring Springs, who was a Miss Hopkins, was born at Waverley. The place now belongs to Lloyd N. Emory.

108

MIDLOTHIAN

BUILT by Mr. Josiah Deans over one hundred sixty years ago, near the head of the North River, Midlothian is a quaint, small, but comfortable home, in Early American style. The building is one room deep, two-stories high, with steep roof and dormer windows.

The parlor and dining room are paneled, and the staircase is built in.

In 1915 this was the home of the Davidsons. Besides them and Mr. Deans, it has been owned by Mr. Charles Talbott, also Mr. Eugene Sanders, of New York. Then Malcolm Matherson, Esq. lived at Midlothian for some years, but after World War I, he sold to Commander and Mrs. Elliott Moorman of Philadelphia. The Moormans still make their home here.

The house faces the river, and there are lovely trees, back and front.

NORTH END

ADJOINING Midlothian, and at the very head of the North River, used to stand North End. The house is long since gone, but it was formerly a Van Bibber estate. "Mrs. Van Bibber, of North End" was the devout congregation of one, who made the responses to Dr. William Taliaferro's readings in Ware Church during the time when there was no minister to conduct the service. Sometimes Mrs. Van Bibber would have to guard against the cold with extra wraps, and a charcoal brazier for her feet.

AUBURN

ON the North River in Mathews County, adjoining Green Plains, Auburn was built in the early 1800's by Philip Tabb for his son, Dr. Henry Wythe Tabb (see Waverley). For many years it remained in his family.

Dr. Henry Wythe Tabb was married three times; first to Hester Van Bibber; from this union there was no issue. His second wide was Martha Tompkins, who left four daughters and one son. His third wife was Ellen Foster, who had three daughters and one son. Henry Wythe Tabb, of Auburn, was born January 12, 1791, died in 1863.

Auburn was originally property of the Mayo family. Mrs. Yeatman, of Auburn, says that her grandfather, Edward Tabb, born February 3, 1719, was the son of John Tabb and Martha Mayo, of Auburn. Records show that John Tabb married Martha Hand. The conclusion is that Martha Hand was a widow who had been Miss Martha Mayo.

Auburn in Georgian style is a magnificent mansion with brick walls

109

three feet thick. The mantels, stairs and panels are of exquisite hand-carved mahogany.

The lawn, with its noble elm trees and excellent river view, is all that could be desired.

This beautiful estate has been lent a special interest by Mr. Joseph Hergeshimer, the famous novelist, who made it the scene of his novel, *Balisand*. White Marsh was supposed to be Welfield in the same story.

During the Civil War the cabinets in the dining room at Auburn were closed up, their keyholes plugged, and their doors made to look like the rest

The great oak at Auburn.

Auburn, the home of Mr. and Mrs. Alexander P. Blood.

The dining room at Auburn.

The hall and stairs at Auburn.

Air view of Green Plains, estate of Mr. and Mrs. Francis Higginson Cabot.

114

of the paneling, to provide a safe hiding place for the family silver.

At one time, Auburn belonged to Mr. and Mrs. Alfred Bell; later to Mr. Charles Heath. It is now the home of Mr. and Mrs. Alexander P. Blood. It is furnished in exquisite taste with beautiful antiques and reproductions, and the library houses a splendid collection of books.

GREEN PLAINS

ON the North River, in Mathews County, stands the large red-brick Georgian house, which Mr. James H. Roy built between 1798 and 1802.

Mr. Roy was the grandson of Dr. Mungo Roy, of Scotland, and the son of Mr. Mungo Roy, of Locust Grove, Caroline County. He married Elizabeth Booth, daughter of George Booth, of Belleville. He was a representative, from Mathews County, in the House of Delegates (1818-1819).

William Henry Roy, the son of James H. and Elizabeth, was also a representative in the House of Delegates (1832-1834). He inherited Green Plains, and was twice married: first to Anne, daughter of Thomas Seddon, of Fredericksburg; then to Euphan, daughter of John MaCrae, of Park Gate, Prince William County. He had two daughters by his first wife. They were Mrs. John C. Rutherfoord, of Rock Castle, and Mrs. Thomas H. Carter, of Pampatike.

By his second wife, he had three daughters; Mrs. Washington and Mrs. Goldsboro, of Maryland, and Mrs. H. McKendree Boyd, of Green Plains.

In 1937 Mr. and Mrs. Higginson Cabot bought Green Plains, and they now reside there. They remodeled and redecorated the house, raising the roof, and setting in dormers; raising the wings, and building large chimneys.

The great central hall, with its magnificent staircase; the deeply recessed windows, with window seats; the chandeliers, the old mantels and paneling; the great fireplaces; the priceless antiques; the handsome oil paintings; the splendid library; all these are only a few of the features which contribute to the beauty and charm of Green Plains. Identical wings built by William H. Roy in 1838 balance each other at the ends of the central building. The two fronts, the towering chimneys, spreading lawn, large old trees and the extensive gardens, go to make a grandeur not often found in Tidewater Virginia.

The river view here is unsurpassed, for Green Plains is on a peninsula, and the blue water sweeps in a semi-circle around the river front.

The garden is enclosed in a scalloped brick wall, four feet high, said to be the only scalloped wall in America. The garden, itself, includes more than an acre, and has a profusion of flowers and shrubs. The tree box is unusually fine, and there are also vast quantities of large and dwarf varieties of box. The crepe myrtles are huge.

Mr. Cabot is quite a farmer and country gentleman, and Mrs. Cabot is a writer.

The great oak and a maze of box at Green Plains.

ON FACING PAGE

Two views of Green Plains. (Above) The river front and (below) the land front showing the great oak in early spring.

The scalloped wall at Green Plains.

ON FACING PAGE

Two views of the garden at Green Plains.

The hall (showing staircase and grandfather's clock) at Green Plains.

The dining room.

The music room.

The drawing room.

ISLEHAM

THE home of Sir John Peyton, the only English baronet who came to live permanently in Virginia, was called Isleham and was situated on the North River near the Mobjack Bay in what is now Mathews County.

Sir John was an officer in the Gloucester Militia. Although an English baronet, during the Revolutionary War he was ardently devoted to the American cause. His descendants intermarried with the best families of Gloucester. The home was an important center of social life in the early days of the county. It was here that Sharpless, the artist, died, and was buried in the family graveyard.

The house has not been restored, but there are still traces of a wide impressive driveway.

Following ownership by its original owner, Sir John, Isleham passed to the Throckmortons and then the Yeatmans.

In 1860 it was the property of Warner T. Throckmorton. Later it was owned by Mr. Mosby, then Dr. Miller.

It is now the property of Miss Alice Corr, of Norfolk, Virginia.

Old records of Isleham show that:

Peter Beverley (died 1728), who was very prominent in the county, married Elizabeth, daughter of Major Robert Peyton, of Isleham; possibly an uncle of Sir John Peyton.

John Dixon, of Mt. Pleasant, Gloucester, married Elizabeth Peyton, of Isleham, February 1773. Their son was John, of Airville. His son, John, a doctor, died unmarried.

December 11, 1773, Major Mordecai Throckmorton married Mary, daughter of Sir John Peyton, of Isleham.

John Patterson, of England, founded Poplar Grove and married Elizabeth Tabb. Their daughter, Elizabeth, married Thomas Robinson Yeatman, of Isleham.

THE SHELTER

IRONICALLY enough, there is now no house on the property called The Shelter, where this famous old house stood for so many years. But because of the mansion's past importance in the social life of Gloucester we wish to include the article, quoted below, lent by Nina Taliaferro Sanders, and written by Philip Hairston Seawell under date of August 29, 1938:

The Shelter, Gloucester County, Va.

THE SHELTER came into the Seawell family of Virginia in the year 1844. At that time it was purchased by Mr. John Tyler Seawell, from Mr. Walter Jones, the father of the late Dr. Walker Jones, and Mr. William P. Jones. The Shelter throughout the long period of its existence was the scene of many happenings that related to the history of Gloucester County, of Virginia, and of the United States.

Part of this historic old homestead stood long before the Revolutionary War, though it is not known who owned it at that time. This early part was an old-styled Dutch gabled-roof building. It formed the nucleus for the later and larger home. The rooms in this part were very large even for the time in which it was built. There was an inside fireplace in the room used later as the dining room when the house came into the possession of the Seawell family. It was in this room that many of the feasts, so customary in the area, took place, here that the tasty dishes for which the Seawell wives were always noted, were served in abundance. In this wing also was another large room, next to the dining room, and an inside-the-house kitchen.

On the second floor were three very large bedchambers.

There was no porch to this building, as was the custom in the section in Pre-Revolutionary days. This house, later a wing of the completed homestead, was two stories in height. The rooms were on different levels. Two steps up or down led to the hall. It is this wing that is the best-known and remembered of the Seawell home because of its distinctive architecture in a country using English Styles. The drive approached the home on this side, from a long lane.

A very old lady, Mrs. Moore, whose husband owned the place before Mr. Jones got it, said that it was used as a hospital during the Revolutionary War. This is most probable, because the house was built long before, and was located about two miles from Gloucester Court House. This placed it in a section in which much action took place during the war.

The main part of the house was added by the same Mr. Jones who turned the historic place over to Mr. John Tyler Seawell. This consisted of a large hallway used as a room, joining a much larger hallway by a flight of several steps. It was this larger hall that became the main entrance hallway and from which the stairs ascended to the bed-chambers.

There was a porch to greet the guest at the front entrance. At the rear of this same hall another small porch let one out into the garden area. From this hall an enormous parlor opened off. This parlor had an inside fireplace. It was here that gay celebrations began and ended,

123

where campaigns were mapped during the Civil War. It was the reception room for the weary traveller, and the ball-room for those gay young peoples of all ages who made up that far-noted Gloucester society.

The Shelter was at the end of a lane a fourth of a mile long. The lane was bordered by heavily shaded woods and crossed a rambling brook. The home got its name from the wife of Mr. Jones. This lane was known far and wide for its roughness, though people always travelled it to get to the Shelter. Mrs. Jones was being taken as a bride to the place, which consisted then of the Dutch wing only. The night was stormy and the bride weary. When she saw the place she is reputed to have said, "Well, it is at least a Shelter." That name has attached and its roofs have sheltered many famous people. Its hospitality was noted so far, that no distance seemed too great to go for its suppers and parties, of which there were many. Many lawyers gathered in its rooms to discuss cases, for it was always the home of a lawyer, when in the Seawell family. It was from here that John Hairston Seawell went off to the University of Va. to study law, and from there to go with his fellow students to the Civil War. Miss Millie Elliott Seawell, the authoress, lived here and drew on the setting of the place for several of her novels. Tho the place was owned by the Seawell family from 1844, only three children of the family were born there, namely, Henrietta, Millie Elliott and John Tyler Seawell, son of John Hairston Seawell, he being the only one of the three now living. This rambling historic house was destroyed by fire in 1925. With it passed a long reign of gayety and sorrow, for it was a house that was old enough to know life.

Philip Hairston Seawell
August 29, 1938

The property now belongs to W. T. Frary Bros.

PART FIVE

ON THE EAST THE PIANKATANK RIVERS IN MATHEWS COUNTY

POPLAR GROVE

THE huge porticoed mansion with wings and many windows, known as Poplar Grove, stands near the East River, in Mathews County, on land which was part of an original grant from George III to Samuel Williams and his son Thomas. They built the oldest part of the present house about 1750.

Mr. John Patterson bought this property some years later, and enlarged and beautified the house. He planted many Lombardy poplars, which were the party symbol of the Whigs—hence the name.

Mr. Patterson was of England, but fought on the American side in the Revolution. He was breveted by Washington at the Battle of Monmouth, and by him recommended for the Navy.

He married Elizabeth Tabb (born July 31, 1760). They left two daughters, Mrs. Thomas Robinson Yeatman, who lived at Isleham, and Mrs. Christopher Tompkins, who lived at Poplar Grove. Her daughter Sally was born here. Mrs. Christopher Tompkins inherited the place, and in turn it became her daughter's home. Sally was a devoted nurse during the Civil War. She was commissioned a captain by General Robert E. Lee; as a captain she could

Poplar Grove, the home of Mrs. George Upton.

126

The tide mill at Poplar Grove.

127

command service and supplies as needed in her work among the wounded. It is said that she was the only woman commissioned by the Confederacy.

In *Tompkins Family,* by Mrs. J. E. Warren, we find some interesting records:

"Maria B. Patterson born Sept. 1794—second wife of Christopher Tompkins."

She had several children: Elizabeth, named for Mr. Tompkins' first wife, Maria, and (Capt.) Sally Louisa, born Nov. 9, 1833. (Sally died 1916.)

Also in *Tompkins Family,* by Mrs. Warren, we find "Married at Poplar Grove 22ond of July 1828 by the Rev. Mr. Cairne, Martha Tabb (daughter of Christopher and Elizabeth Tompkins) to Dr. Henry W. Tabb, son of Philip and Mary Tabb."

One of the few tide mills left in America is at Poplar Grove. During the Revolution, meal was ground here for Washington's troops. It is said that thirty-two bushels of meal could be ground on a tide. During the Civil War, the mill was burned by the Northern soldiers, but it was rebuilt and used until after the beginning of this century.

The gardens, the serpentine walls, similar to those at the University of Virginia, and the grove, are outstanding features at Poplar Grove, and combine to lend distinction to the place.

Poplar Grove has belonged to the Brown family, to Judge J. Taylor Garnett, and to the Butler family.

Mrs. George Upton, who bought the estate from the Butlers in 1927, still makes it her home.

The house is built on different levels. We find lovely paneling in the west wing, which is the oldest part. The center was the next part to be added. Mrs. Upton has the place nicely furnished in reproductions and antiques. The land now consists of two thousand acres.

HOPEMONT

HIGH on a hill, on the Piankatank River, nine miles from the Chesapeake, stands Hopemont. It is a brick Georgian house and was built about 1750 by the Fritchett family. At that time it was called Providence. Later (in 1799), Providence was owned by the Howletts, who renamed it Howlett Hall.

In 1936 Mr. and Mrs. McComb bought and restored the house, adding one wing. They again called it Providence. The house is noted for its fine paneling.

The garden was originally laid out by an eminent English botanist. It is now being restored by the present owners, Mr. and Mrs. Hope Norton.

With its end chimneys, the third story dormer windows; and classical

128

Hopemont, the home of Mr. and Mrs. Hope Norton.

Gate at Hopemont, showing brick wall with eagles on gateposts.

130

Main entrance of Hopemont.

131

The garden entrance to Hopemont.

132

Fan steps at Hopemont.

133

On this and the facing page are views of the garden at Hopemont.

134

A remnant at Hesse.

136

doorway, with fan steps, Hopemont has preserved the purity of its architecture. The columns of the portico ascend from the bricked terrace floor to the second story roof. In restoring the fences, walls and outbuildings, the Nortons are exercising the most punctilious care in developing and preserving the correct surroundings for this architectural gem.

HESSE

WILLIAM ARMISTEAD, the emigrant, was the builder of Hesse. His son, the Honorable John Armistead, was a member of His Majesty's Council in the latter part of the 17th century.

King Carter, of Corotoman, married Judith Armistead, of Hesse.

John's son, Henry, married Martha, daughter of the Honorable Lewis Burwell. She had been a great belle, with many suitors. Governor Sir Francis Nicholson had paid court to her, but she refused his hand. Sir Francis had said that if she ever married anyone else three murders would be committed immediately: that of the bride-groom; that of the officiating minister; and that of the justice who issued the license!

Martha and Henry had three children, first Lucy, who married "Secretary" Thomas Nelson (1716-1782), son of Thomas Nelson the emigrant; second, Martha, wife of Dudley Digges, who was a member of the first Executive Council of the State of Virginia; and finally William Armistead, who succeeded his father as owner of Hesse, and who married Mary, daughter of James Bowles, of Maryland. He died in 1755.

In 1765 William's son, William II, married Maria, daughter of Charles Carter, of Cleve by his second wife, Anne, daughter of William Byrd II.

There is on record some interesting correspondence between Maria and her relatives, the Byrds, of Westover.

She named her son Charles Byrd Armistead. When he died in 1797, he left no descendants, so the big old house of Hesse with 3877 acres of land passed from the Armistead family.

For a number of years the place was deserted, the house neglected and desolate, but the present owners, Mr. and Mrs. John Maxwell, are considering restoration of this fine old mansion. There has been an architect's drawing of tentative plans for the restoration. According to these plans the grandeur of Hesse will be restored, too. All that is left now appears bleak and discouraging, but in its heyday Hesse was an imposing place.

Standing high on the banks of the Piankatank, with terraced gardens reaching down to the water's edge, Hesse extended hospitality to the finest families of Virginia. Hither came the Wormeleys, the Burwells, the Carters, the Byrds, the Cookes, the Whitings, the Booths, and the Pages. Hesse was a Georgian house with end chimneys, and was built of brick. There was a frame wing and small front porch.

It is said that the brick walls at the foundation were nine feet thick, and the rest of the old house of corresponding solidity. Now the most of the old house has been destroyed, and the terraced gardens washed away by the waters of the river.

But Hesse has made its imprint on the state and the nation. Many Americans from all parts of the country can boast with justifiable pride of their ancestors, the Armisteads, of Hesse, and many prideful eyes will come to see the mansion—after the restoration.

KINGSTON HALL

IN Mathews County, on the road from Gloucester Court House, is the magnificent home of Mr. and Mrs. George C. Kirkmyer.

The original house was built in 1730, by Thomas Smith, on a grant named Centerville. The large center building was added by George Tabb, in 1840. The wings were built a hundred years later, by the present owners, who named the place Kingston Hall.

Historically, Kingston Hall is noted for being the birthplace of two Phi Beta Kappa founders, Thomas and Armistead Smith, who were sons of the builder. This place, formerly called Woodstock, was long the home of the Lane family, a member of which was Dr. Thomas B. Lane, the famous Confederate surgeon.

Standing back in a beautiful grove, with its many gables, its vast array of windows, and classic front, Kingston Hall is a magnificent sight. The driveway, the old trees, the wide stretches of lawn are most impressive. The profusion of flowers and shrubs add to the charm of the grounds.

The paneling of the interior has been much admired, and the great staircase with its unique railing is very unusual. The railing has five balusters to each step.

WINDSOR

WINDSOR, on the line between Gloucester and Mathews Counties, has almost disappeared, but it was once famous as home of John Clayton, the colonial botanist, who was the friend and correspondent of many learned scientists in different parts of the world. Mr. Clayton was for fifty years Clerk of the county.

He studied many plants native to Virginia, or imported into the state.

138

Gateway to Kingston Hall.

Kingston Hall, home of Mr. and Mrs. George Kirkmyer.

Kingston Hall, showing trees and flowers at front.

Kingston Hall, view from the back, showing gables and chimneys.

142

The famed staircase at Kingston Hall.

The traces of his elaborate and extensive botanical gardens can still be discerned.

Mr. Clayton wrote, in collaboration with the Dutch botanist, Gronovius, *Flora Virginica,* published at Leyden in 1743.

Among John Clayton's friends were numbered Peter Kalm, of Finland, Linnaeus, of Sweden, Alexander Gardner, of England, Thomas Jefferson, William Byrd and Benjamin Franklin.

The Garden Club has put up a marker at Windsor, honoring Clayton, and is considering making a shrine there. It is only very recently that we have awakened to the fact that Clayton ranks with Liberty Hyde Bailey, of Cornell, and other famous botanists.

SEAFORD

FROM Mrs. F. Snowden Hopkins' account in the *Baltimore Sun* of August 27, 1933, of the Piankatank and vicinity, we find that Seaford was on the creek bank inland from the Piankatank. She says that at that time there was left only —a tree-box avenue, a few magnificent elms, and an overgrown garden.

She speaks of ruins—no house left. Seaford was originally the Tabb home —not far from Mathews Court House.

From old records we find that Thomas Tabb married Elizabeth Teackle, of the Eastern Shore, and lived at Seaford. He became the ancestor of many "Seaford Tabbs."

KENWOOD

KENWOOD, the home of Mr. Norman Cook, while not very old, has some historic interest and a pleasant location. The house itself has traditional and architectural value.

THE HAVEN

THE HAVEN figured in the shipping of the early days and also was a refuge for our ships in times of naval engagements along the coast.

HAVEN'S EDGE

HAVEN'S EDGE, the handsome home of Colonel Fales, which is nearby, played, to a certain extent, a similar role.

Kenwood, home of Mr. Norman Cook.

145

Kenwood, view from the back.

ON FACING PAGE

Two views of Colonel Pales's home, Haven's Edge.

Roaring Springs, the home of Mr. and Mrs. R. M. Janney.

PART SIX
AWAY FROM THE RIVERS

ROARING SPRINGS

IN Gloucester County off Route 17 onto Road 616 one finds the old Colonial house known as Roaring Springs.

It was built by James Baytop Taliaferro, at, or near the end of the 18th century and in early years it was the seat of the Taliaferro family.

Built on simple Dutch-Colonial lines, with gambrel roof, the interior is beautiful, with its fine paneling and woodwork.

It is, as Anne Page Johns, the Richmond poet, so aptly puts it,—"A sequestered small country manor-house of old-time charm, projected into its useful present."

There are about twelve acres of park and lawn in the grounds, and the elm trees are impressively beautiful.

Paintings from the Johns Hopkins collection, priceless family heirlooms, and outstanding antique furniture decorate this charming farm home.

Roaring Springs is owned by Mrs. R. M. Janney.

BELLE FARM

ALTHOUGH this treatise is of the old houses as they are in the 1950's, we have thought it important to bring in some houses, occasionally, that at this time are only history, legend or tradition, and not "four walls" any more; in short, houses that have been dismantled or destroyed.

Such a house is, or at any rate was, Belle Farm. General William Booth

Taliaferro mentions it as a pre-Revolutionary and colonial home of Gloucester.

Mrs. Maria Edwards writes that Belle Farm, the residence of Colonel Lewis, was the scene of the large dinner party when her grandfather, John Seawell, was proposed as a candidate for the Legislature. The grandfather was a Federalist, but his son, John, who went to William and Mary, returned a Democrat. The votes were taken and her father (John Seawell II) refused to vote for his father, whereupon the latter immediately declined the proposal to nominate him, declaring he would not consent to run if his own son opposed him.

Notes from the records of the Tabb family and their connections, say that Ellen Deans, daughter of Josiah Lilly Deans, married Fielding L. Taylor, of Belle Farm, and had two children, Fielding Lewis (died) and Ellen Y. Deans.

Roaring Springs, house and garden.

The living room at Roaring Springs.

A marriage announcement from the *Virginia Magazine of History and Genealogy* says that Robert Thruston and Sarah Brown were married at Belle Farm in Gloucester County, Virginia, by the Rev. Mr. Smith, December 22, 1804.

Mrs. M. M. Taliaferro (a granddaughter of Robert Munford), in a letter, written in 1895, says that after the death of her grandfather in Charles City County, her grandmother removed to Belle Farm, Gloucester County, at which place her sons, Samuel and Robert died, and lie buried. Belle Farm was owned at the time she moved there by her brother-in-law, Mr. Fielding Lewis, "and my grandmother continued to reside there with her daughter and only remaining child, Margaret Ann Munford, until that daughter (who

151

was my mother) married Mr. John Sinclair, my father, when she went to live with them at Shabby Hall, which my father afterwards sold to Mr. Robert C. Selden, whose widow still resides there, as you know." (Shabby Hall is now Sherwood.)

Mrs. Sally Robins says in 1893, in telling of the destruction of the last old brick mansion in Gloucester town, that "From this house, built by an early colonist named Thruston, whose widow married a Lewis and then a Tabb, two curiously-carved mantel-pieces were carried to the Belle Farm; and this old Lewis home still holds them, together with one of the rarest collections of china, silver and glass, portraits and jewels (heirlooms of the Warners, the Lewises, the Corbins and the Taylors) which this county contains."

Waterman says (in *Mansions of Virginia*) "making the pediment traverse the length of the plan was shown to be undesirable at Belle Farm in Gloucester, where the effect was ungainly in the extreme."

Belle Farm, now the property of Mr. and Mrs. John L. Lewis, Jr., has been dismantled, reassembled and rebuilt on Indian Springs Road, in Williamsburg, and it seems to nestle into its new surroundings, as though it had been there all along. It is a clapboard house, with center hall, and large rooms on each side. Both these rooms have open fireplaces, and paneling about shoulder high. The parlor, or in today's vernacular, the living room, has arches opening into recesses, on each side of the fireplace, and in the back of these recesses are windows, with tiny diamond-shaped panes of glass.

At the end of the center hall, there is a cross hall in which, as at Tuckahoe, is the staircase leading to the second floor. Straight across from the door of the center hall is the door to the dining room. This room also has an open fireplace, and the fine woodwork has carving to represent scenes from Aesop's Fables.

At Belle Farm there is boxwood, other shrubbery, a beginning of a flower garden, and a nice vegetable garden.

Mr. Lewis is a descendant (about the tenth generation) of Augustine Warner, of Warner Hall; and of John Lewis, who married Mr. Warner's granddaughter, and he is also a cousin of George Washington, Robert E. Lee, England's Queen Mother, and of her Majesty, Queen Elizabeth II.

GLOUCESTER PLACE

GLOUCESTER PLACE, a large old house which used to stand on the "Gloucestertowne" Road was important in the early days of Gloucester. It was built by John Seawell, a large importing merchant, and was the Seawell home for some years.

Gloucester Place was also the former residence of President John Tyler.

MARLFIELD

MARLFIELD, in the upper end of the county, was built early in the 18th century, by the Buckners. It was a T-shaped brick house. The first printing press in Virginia was brought to Gloucester County by John Buckner, who was Clerk of the county. Lord Culpeper, the governor, reproved him in 1682 for having printed, without license, the laws of 1680. Further printing was prohibited, and some say his press was destroyed.

Marlfield had a center hall, with a room on each side, downstairs and up, this being only the four big rooms, and the two halls, at the time it came into the Catesby Jones family. Mr. Catesby G. Jones, of Gloucester, tells us that it was bought by his great-great-great-grandfather in 1779 or 1780. The purchaser immediately built a wing in the center back, thus making the building T-shaped. The new part also had large rooms, which were used as dining room and kitchen. In 1904 Mr. Jones's family sold Marlfield to Mr. Z. T. Gray. This made about a century and a quarter that the Joneses lived at Marlfield, and during that time it was one of the social centers of the county. The large chimneys, open fireplaces, lovely staircase, mantels, and paneling were typical of the period.

There was a large amount of timber on the place when Mr. Gray bought it; in fact, that was why he bought the place. He sold large quantities of timber, but today, there still remain at Marlfield, some fine trees.

The grounds are over-grown, the house is in ruins, and the old graveyard, with its fine old vaults and tombstones, is also over-grown. Here lie the ancestors of the Jones family, and also of the Buckners.

CLIFFORD

ON Route 17, between Gloucester and Gloucester Point, one and a half miles from the Court House, stands Clifford, the old home of the Kemp family, of Gloucester County. Miss Mary Kemp, of Richmond, tells us that a unique thing about Clifford was that, in olden days, each bedroom had its own staircase leading up to it from the room below. She said, however, that when the home was remodeled in recent years, all the staircases except two were removed.

The house is of frame construction, and of the Colonial structure, Miss Kemp says, only the old parlor and dining room remain. In her childhood,

153

Fiddlers Green, the home of the Hutchesons.

seventy years ago, there were the most beautiful flowers in her mother's garden, and magnificent shrubs, which were ancient even at that time. Miss Kemp also recalls the trees, huge, century-old, of different varieties, but among them many walnut trees.

The proprietors of the Antique Shoppe in Gloucester now own Clifford. How they must enjoy it!

FIDDLERS GREEN

FIDDLERS GREEN, the birthplace of Ruth Nelson Robins Gordon (Mrs. Thomas C. Gordon), of Richmond, is not far from Gloucester Court House. It was here her father returned after the War Between the States, when all seemed lost. It was here her mother, Sally Nelson Robins, the illustrious writer, lived.

The house, built late in the seventeenth century, is two-storied, with shingle roof and dormer windows, has large end chimneys and a porch all

154

across the front. After the death of Mrs. Gordon's father, the family removed to Richmond, and Fiddlers Green passed into other hands.

The charming old place is now the home of the Hutchesons.

WALTER REED BIRTHPLACE

ON the road from Gloucester to Cappahosic, one passes near the forks of the roads a tiny three-room white house. Here the greatly beloved Walter Reed was born September 13, 1851. This place is called Belroi. Walter Reed's

Birth place of Walter Reed, Belroi.

Long Bridge Ordinary.

father, a minister, had lost his home by fire, a few weeks previously, and the family found temporary refuge here. Dr. Walter Reed was one of Gloucester's most noted sons. It was he who made long and tedious, as well as dangerous, experiments until at last he discovered the cause of yellow fever. He died in Washington at the age of fifty-one. It is for him that the great Walter Reed Hospital, at Washington, was named. The people of Gloucester have honored his memory, and it is hoped that Belroi will become a national shrine.

LONG BRIDGE ORDINARY

AT Gloucester Court House, Long Bridge Ordinary, a hostelry famous in Colonial days, is still much in the mind of the public. It was built as early, certainly, as 1727. From here a coach service to Fredericksburg was regularly maintained at least from 1736 on. A poster dated that year hangs in Rising

156

Sun Tavern in Fredericksburg announcing the departure of the stage coach in the morning for Hornets Nest, and Long Bridge Ordinary.

Although this building has only one chimney, it has five fireplaces. Built on a hillside, the garden entrance is into the basement which has a hall, dining room, and kitchen. The first floor, entered at front from hilltop level, has a hall, a large living room, and a powder room, the second-floor a hall and a bedroom where the proprietor slept. The staircase is classically plain, and is sometimes called a platform stairs.

The lower story of the house is of brick, and the upper two stories of wood. The door panels were doubled, with the grain of the wood of the outer panels running straight, and the inner panels slanting. This was to turn the point of the Indian's arrows.

Many distinguished guests have eaten at Long Bridge Ordinary.

Around the beginning of the present century this place changed hands several times.

This may have been due to the fact that with the beginning of the automobile era, Long Bridge Ordinary lost its value as a hostelry.

In 1914, the Gloucester Woman's Club acquired the property by purchase. With the house they bought one and a quarter acres of land. The garden is being beautifully restored under the supervision of Mrs. Edward Newton Cheek.

GLOUCESTER COURT HOUSE

THE present Gloucester Court House was built in 1766, the previous building on this site having been destroyed by fire.

It is of lovely colonial architecture, with brick arches, and white-columned porch. The porch was added after the Revolution. The records of Gloucester have been destroyed three times—the last time when Richmond was burned during the evacuation of the city in the Civil War.

The town of Gloucester, at that time called Botetourt, was laid out in 1769. In olden days great leniency was practised in the keeping of prisoners. Each day near the middle of the day, they were allowed to take a walk from the Gloucester jail to get their exercise. A tall tree about a mile away was the furthest point to which they were permitted to go. No one ever heard of trouble with escapees, but of course the most of them were in for debt!

The interior of the Court House is not only fitted out in the best taste but is also most unusual, and of great historic and sentimental interest. In the courtroom are forty-eight portraits and seven tablets commemorating the great of the county. Among the forty-eight are two portraits of General William Booth Taliaferro, of Belleville, and one of Dr. Walter Reed.

157

Gloucester Court House with monument and green.

One tablet has been put up (by the Gloucester Monument Association) to the Women of Gloucester County, Virginia, during the Civil War, 1861-65—; another to the distinguished men of the Page family; and one to the illustrious Cookes, four of whom had Mordecai as their given names.

There is a tablet to the memory of Dr. Walter Reed, one to Nathaniel Bacon, one to John M. Gregory, Governor of Virginia and Judge of Circuit Court, and one in "Honor of the men of Gloucester, who on land and sea, in field, camp and air, gave themselves and their services to our County."

For a complete list of the portraits, and of the texts of the inscriptions on the tablets, see *Twelve Virginia Counties*, by John H. Gwathmey.

Mr. Gwathmey gives, too, a list of officers of the five companies of infantry and the three of cavalry that went into the War Between the States from Gloucester. He also lists officers from Gloucester who were attached to other commands.

An entire roll of Confederate soldiers from Gloucester is to be found in the Clerk's office.

The circular Court Green, with its group of quaint, beautiful buildings, divides the road. It is a lovely place. The brick wall which surrounds it was built by the Gloucester Garden Club, which was founded in June, 1928, by Mrs. George Mackubin, Mrs. H. O. Sanders and Mrs. William Fleet Taliaferro. The design for the wall was executed by a Williamsburg architect, and W. P. A. labor was used in its construction. Then, also under Williamsburg advice, the walks from one building to another were laid out in patterns in keeping with the period of the buildings, and the Court Green was further beautified. Besides the Court house, there are the Clerk's Office, a brick structure built in 1890; the Old Debtor's Prison, adjoining the Court house (from which the prisoners used to take their noon walk), which dates from early in the eighteenth century; and the tiny Old Clerk's Office, which is also of brick, and was built in 1821. Nowhere in Virginia is there a group of court buildings more attractive, or grounds more lovely than at Gloucester.

WARE CHURCH

NEAR the head of the Ware River and not far from the old "War Path" or "Indian Road," stands Ware Church, the old brick rectangular building where citizens of Gloucester County have worshiped for nearly three hundred years. An earlier building, called The Glebe, stood on the peninsula known as Glen Roy. The present building is on land given by the Throckmorton family of Church Hill, and it was completed soon after 1690. The grove of original growth trees which surround the church consists of cedars, pines, oaks, elms and other varieties usually found in virgin growth of this section.

Gloucester Court House, closeup.

These trees, with the old brick wall which surrounds the church, the old part of the church yard and the quaint old tombstones, with their interesting inscriptions, all evoke the atmosphere of another world, one long since vanished into the past.

The church building has been little changed, just enough for comfort for the congregation. The old box pews which were used by the British for horse stalls during the Revolution, have been replaced by more modern ones. A polished floor now covers the stones upon which once congregations walked and knelt. Lights have been installed, but the fixtures are of Colonial design.

Many generations have buried their dead at Ware Church. The cemetery has had to be enlarged from time to time. It is interesting to note that in each generation the church roll in the clerk's book reads like a list of names from the tombstones outside. The descendants keep the faith, even to this day.

Many persons were buried under the chancel of Ware in early times. Their tombstones are still there. Among those so interred were the Rev. J. R. Fox, Rector of Ware, his wife and child, and the child's nurse; Mrs. Francis Willis; the Rev. John Richards, who died in 1735, and his wife Amy Richards, (1725) and her maid, Mary Ades, who died two days after her mistress.

The very ancient Ware communion service is part of a set presented originally by Augustine Warner to Petsworth Church. When church services were no longer held at Ware, this communion service was preserved and cared for by Mrs. Mary Cooke Booth Jones, the widow of the Rev. Emmanuel Jones; the two chalices and patens were given to the Rev. Mr. Cairns, Rector of Ware, on the night of the marriage of Mr. Jones' granddaughter, Lucy Ann Jones, to George Wythe Booth, of Belleville; the tankard had been lost by the Rev. Emmanuel Jones; a later tankard has been given to Ware by the Rev. Emmanuel Jones' descendants to replace the one he lost.

The building at Ware is a perfect rectangle, forty by eighty feet. The bricks were made in the brickyard west of the church property, and were laid by local bricklayers, with English artisans to glaze the brick ends. The present roof is slate, put on in 1854. The rafters, of hand-riven oak, are twelve by eighteen inches, and were found to be in perfect condition when the roof was replaced.

According to English and American architectural authorities, Ware Church is perfect in its simplicity. The main door is to the west, with the chancel in the east end of the building. There are cross aisles from the north and south, and a cross aisle in the rear of the nave, with two longitudinal aisles extending from this to the chancel.

Each of the twelve large windows is surmounted by an arch. The five windows on each side have thirty-eight panes each, while the two double ones over the chancel have sixty panes each.

Heavy wooden uprights and cross-sections make perfect crosses in each window.

The foundation walls begin six feet below the surface, and are five feet thick to ground level. From ground level to a height of three feet the walls are four feet thick; above that they are three feet thick. The doors are constructed of two layers of wood; each layer is an inch thick, the grain of the wood in one of the layers runs crosswise to the grain in the other. This was a precaution against Indian arrows.

Ware Church.

162

Ware Church, interior.

163

At times in the past there was no minister, but almost always, with the exception of ten years prior to 1826, so the Reverend William Byrd Lee (who wrote the history of Ware Church for *The Southern Churchman* early in this century) avers, a minister came in soon after a vacancy occurred. He says ". . . it appears there was a minister generally at hand to administer baptism, and other rites of the Church."

During one period, when the church had no rector, Dr. William Taliaferro went faithfully every Sunday morning to read the prayers and lessons and Psalms of the service, while the lone member of the congregation, "old" Mrs. Van Bibber, of North End, made the responses. Bishop Meade comments on the devout spiritual character of these two saintly people.

The Reverend Mr. Lee speaks of the high regard in which the ministers of Ware were held by their congregation (as shown by tablets, tomb inscriptions, etc.), and he lists the following as examples of long tenure in the service, in Gloucester and Mathews:

"Mr. Clack served nearly 45 years
Mr. Gwynn, 16; Rev. Guy Smith, 18;
Rev. Emmanuel Jones (in Petsworth) 39;
Rev. Mr. Hughes, 25; Mr. Mann, 40;
and the present pastor 25 years."

"The present pastor" that Mr. Lee referred to, was himself; and his "25 years" eventually became forty years of service, after which he retired and became Rector Emeritus.

The roll of the vestry of Ware, like that of Abingdon, is a list of the names of truly great Americans.

The interest and earnest work of the congregation under the auspices of the Chancel Guild, have effected the restoration and beautification of the interior of the church, and through munificent gifts, several memorials have been erected.

ABINGDON CHURCH

ON the road from Gloucester Court House to Gloucester Point, about six miles from The Point, stands Abingdon Church. It is cruciform in style, built of rose brick, and is said to have been planned by Sir Christopher Wren. The building is eighty-one feet long, and seventy-six and a half feet wide. The eastern and western ends of the "cross" measure thirty-six feet in width on the outside, while the northern and southern outside ends of the cross measure

Abingdon Church, showing wall.

165

thirty-five feet. The walls are in Flemish bond with glazed heads. They are two feet thick.

The silver service still in use was presented by Major Lewis Burwell, of Carter's Creek in 1703. A smaller building preceded the present one, but it seems a little difficult to determine the exact date of the building of either. It is perhaps safe to say the earlier church was built about the middle of the 1600's, and the present church about one hundred years later. William Byrd, of Westover, said of the old church ". . . exquisite little church, the finest I have seen in the country."

It is a fact, however, that much of the original woodwork of the previous building was retained in the present edifice. A distinguished pediment tops the west doorway, which is superb in its symmetry and grace. There is an old flagstone pathway leading to the door.

The Warners, of Warner Hall, gave the land on which the church was built. The family, including Mildred, who married Lawrence Washington and became George Washington's grandmother, attended church here.

Some of the old box pews were used by the British as box stalls for horses during the Revolution. After the Civil War they were removed and replaced by the high-backed pews now in use.

Some of the tombstones in the Abingdon Cemetery have coats of arms carved on them. The cemetery has been enlarged from time to time, and names on the stones are known throughout the county.

Within the churchyard, close to the front door, are handsome "table" style tombstones of the Burwells; one of the family moved to Abingdon from the old Burwell home, Carter's Creek. One of the tombstones is in memory of Mrs. Burwell, who persisted in calling herself "Lady Berkeley," even on the tombstone, though her husband, Governor Berkeley, had died some years before she married Mr. Nathaniel Burwell.

The chancel is in the east end of the cross. Here was placed, probably in the early 1840's, the beautiful pentagonal reredos which still is much admired. It was nicely described by Mrs. Fielding Lewis Taylor in these words:

> "It represents the facade of a Greek temple in the bas-relief, about twenty feet in height and extending entirely across the back of the chancel. It is handsomely carved, and painted snowy white. Straight across the lintel of the facade runs the first line of the Te Deum, 'We praise Thee, O God.' The roof of the reredos dividing at the apex, supports a pine apple both in high relief. Between the four fluted pilasters of the reredos are set four long black tablets, framed and lettered in gold. These contain the Creed, the Lord's Prayer, and the

166

Abingdon Church, within wall.

167

Abingdon Church, interior.

Ten Commandments. Alas, the breath of time has dimmed the beautiful words. The light from the great arched windows (in the head of the cruciform building, on either side of the chancel) shines full upon these four foundation pillars of the Faith once delivered to the saints. The effect of the whole is simple, but beautiful, full of deep spiritual earnestness."

Above the apex of the reredos is a gilt cross painted on glass.

The main aisle from the west door to the chancel is crossed by the aisles from the north and south entrances. In olden days the Thruston and Lewis families occupied the gallery in the south arm of the cross, and the Burwells and Pages occupied the one in the north arm. Servants sat in seats placed back of their masters.

Of course a modern furnace heats Abingdon in cold weather now, but in an older day, heated bricks, braziers and warm clothing had to be depended on for warmth.

Near the beginning of this century Mr. Joseph Bryan enclosed the church yard, consisting of about two and a half acres, in an attractive and substantial brick wall. This adds to the impressive beauty of the old church surrounded by the grove of lovely old trees and the tombstones.

In a book called *Virginia Colonial Churches,* second edition, published by The Southern Churchman Company in 1908 in Richmond, Virginia, is the most complete history of "Abingdon Church, Gloucester County, Virginia," that we have been able to find. It is written by the Reverend William Byrd Lee, Rector. Mr. Lee used all sources available, and authenticity of the facts he gives are self-evident. He says that, according to the report of the Reverend Thomas Hughes to the Bishop of London, in 1724, "there were three hundred families in the parish; that services were held every Lord's Day, Good Friday and Christmas, in the forenoon; that there were sixty or seventy communicants; that the Holy Communion was administered three times a year, and that about two hundred Christians generally attended the church."

Mr. Lee goes on to give, as far as possible, a complete list of ministers, wardens and vestrymen of Abingdon. He gives total counts of baptisms, and ends with a list of five hundred seventy surnames of resident families of Abingdon Parish, Gloucester County, Virginia from 1677 to 1761.

BIBLIOGRAPHY

Virginia, a Guide to the Old Dominion. Compiled by Workers of the Writers' Program of the Works Projects Administration in the State of Virginia. New York, 1940. Oxford University Press.

Andrews, Matthew Page. *Virginia, the Old Dominion.* Richmond, 1949. The Dietz Press.

Brock, Henry Irving. *Colonial Churches in Virginia.* Richmond, 1930. The Dale Press.

Byrd, William, of Westover. *Another Secret Diary.* Edited by Maude Woodfin, decoded by Marion Tingling. Richmond, 1942. The Dietz Press.

Byrd, William, of Westover. *Secret Diary.* Edited by Louis Wright and Marion Tingling. Richmond, 1941. The Dietz Press.

Chamberlayne, C. G. *The Vestry Book of Petsworth Parish, Gloucester County, Virginia.* 1677-1793. Transcribed, Annotated and Indexed by C. G. Chamberlayne. Richmond, 1933. The Library Board.

Chandler, Joseph Everett. *The Colonial Architecture of Maryland, Pennsylvania and Virginia.* Boston, 1892. Bates, Kimball & Guild.

Christian, Frances Archer & Massie, Susanne Williams, Editors. *Homes and Gardens in Old Virginia.* Revised Edition. Richmond, 1950. Garrett and Massie, Inc.

Coffin, Lewis A., Jr. & Holden, Arthur C. *Brick Architecture of the Colonial Period in Maryland & Virginia.* New York, 1919. Architectural Book Publishing Company, Inc.

Colonial Churches of Virginia. Richmond, 1908. The Southern Churchman Company.

Davis, Deering, with Dorsey, Stephen P. and Hall, Ralph Cole. Special Article by Nancy McClelland. *Alexandria Houses.* 1946. Architectural Book Publishing Company, Inc.

Davis, Deering. *Annapolis Houses, 1700-1775.* 1947. Architectural Book Publishing Company, Inc.

Davis, Deering with Dorsey, Stephen P. and Hall, Ralph Cole. *Georgetown Houses of the Federal Period, Washington, D.C. 1780-1830.* 1944. Architectural Book Publishing Company, Inc.

Department of Agriculture and Immigration of the State of Virginia, George W. Koiner, Commissioner. *A Handbook of Virginia.* Richmond, 1909. Everett Waddey Company, Printers.

Eberlein, Harold Donaldson. *The Architecture of Colonial America.* Boston, 1915. Little, Brown & Company.

Elliott, Charles Wyllys. *The Book of American Interiors.* Boston, 1876. James R. Osgood & Company.

Forman, Henry Chandlee. *The Architecture of the Old South, The Medieval Style, 1585-1850.* Cambridge, Mass., 1948. Harvard University Press.

Forman, Henry Chandlee. *Jamestown and St. Mary's, Buried Cities of Romance.* Baltimore, 1938. The Johns Hopkins Press.

Frary, I. T. *Early American Doorways.* Richmond, 1937. Garrett and Massie.

Frary, I. T. *Thomas Jefferson, Architect and Builder,* Third Edition. Richmond, 1950. Garrett and Massie.

Freeman, Douglas Southall. *George Washington.* New York & London, 1948. Charles Scribners Sons.

Freeman, Douglas Southall. *R. E. Lee.* New York & London, 1934. Charles Scribners Sons.

French, Leigh, Jr. *Colonial Interiors.* New York, 1923. William Helburn, Inc.

Gloucester County, Virginia. *Educational Survey Report.* Richmond, 1928. State Board of Education.

Gwathmey, John H. *Historical Register of Virginians in the Revolution, Soldiers, Sailors, Marines, 1775-1783.* Richmond, 1938. The Dietz Press.

Gwathmey, John H. *Legends of Virginia Courthouses.* Richmond, 1933. The Dietz Press.

Gwathmey, John H. *Legends of Virginia Lawyers.* Richmond, 1934. The Dietz Press.

Gwathmey, John H. *Twelve Virginia Counties.* Richmond, 1937. The Dietz Press.

Hamlin, Talbot. *Greek Revival Architecture in America.* London, New York, Toronto, 1944. Oxford University Press.

Hergesheimer, Joseph. *Balisand.* New York, 1924. Alfred A. Knopf.

Historic American Buildings Survey. Washington, 1941. National Park Service.

Howells, John Mead. *Lost Examples of Colonial Architecture.* New York, 1931. William Helburn, Inc.

Huntley, Elizabeth Valentine. *Peninsula Pilgrimage.* Richmond, 1941. The Press of Whittet & Shepperson.

Jackson, Joseph. *American Colonial Architecture.* Philadelphia, 1924. David McKay Company.

Johnston, Frances Benjamin and Waterman, Thomas Tileston. *The Early Architecture of North Carolina.* Chapel Hill, 1941-1947. University of North Carolina Press.

Johnston, George Ben, M.D. *Some Medical Men of Mark from Virginia.* Richmond, 1905. Reprinted from the *Old Dominion Journal of Medicine and Surgery.*

Lancaster, Robert A., Jr. *Historic Virginia Homes and Churches.* Philadelphia and London, 1915. J. B. Lippincott Company.

Lee, Mrs. Marguerite du Pont. *Virginia Ghosts and Others.* Richmond, 1932. The William Byrd Press, Inc.

Legg, Carrie Mason. Unpublished Manuscript. Elmington.

Library of Congress. *Colonial Churches in the Original Colony of Virginia.* Washington, D.C. U. S. Government Printing Office.

Mason, Polly Cary. *Records of Colonial Gloucester County, Virginia,* Volume I. Compiled by Polly Cary Mason. Newport News, Virginia, 1946. Mrs. George C. Mason. Post Office Box 720.

Mason, Polly Cary. *Records of Colonial Gloucester County, Virginia,* Volume II. Compiled by Polly Cary Mason. Newport News, Virginia, 1948. Mrs. George C. Mason, Post Office Box 720.

Massie, Susanne Williams and Christian, Frances Archer, Editors. *Homes and Gardens of Virginia.* With an Introduction by Douglas S. Freeman. Richmond, 1931. Garrett & Massie, Inc.

Meade, William, bp. 1789-1862. *Old Churches, Ministers and Families of Virginia.* Philadelphia, 1872. J. B. Lippincott & Company. Reprinted, Lippincott, 1931. Two volumes with Wise Index. First published 1857. Second edition 1861.

Moore, Virginia. *Virginia Is a State of Mind.* New York, 1942. E. P. Dutton and Company, Inc.

Mumford, Lewis. *The South in Architecture.* New York, 1941. Harcourt, Brace & Company.

Nutting, Wallace. *Virginia Beautiful.* Framingham, Massachusetts, 1930. Old America Company.

Paxton, Annabel. *Washington Doorways.* Richmond, 1940. The Dietz Press.

Rawson, Marion Nicholl. *Sing, Old House.* New York, 1934. E. P. Dutton & Company, Inc.

Robins, Sally Nelson. *Gloucester, One of the First Chapters of the Commonwealth of Virginia; History of Gloucester County, Virginia, and Its Families.* Illustrated with Photographs by Miss Blanche Dimmock, of Sherwood. Richmond, 1893. West, Johnston & Company.

Rothery, Agnes. *New Roads in Old Virginia.* Revised Edition. Boston and New York, 1937. Houghton Mifflin Company.

Rothery, Agnes. *Virginia The New Dominion.* New York, London, 1940. D. Appleton-Century Company.

Sale, Edith Tunis. *Boxwood and Terraced Gardens of Virginia.* Richmond, 1925. The William Byrd Press, Inc.

Sale, Edith Tunis, Editor. *Historic Gardens of Virginia.* Compiled by the James River Garden Club Committee: Edith Tunis Sale, Laura C. Martin Wheelwright, Juanita Massie Patterson, Lila. L. Williams, Caroline Coleman Duke. Foreword by Mary Johnston. Richmond, 1925. The William Byrd Press, Inc.

Sale, Mrs. Edith Dabney (Tunis). *Interiors of Virginia Houses of Colonial Times.* Richmond, 1927. The William Byrd Press, Inc.

Sale, Edith Tunis. *Manors of Virginia in Colonial Times.* Philadelphia and London, 1909. J. B. Lippincott Company.

Scott, Mary Wingfield. *Houses of Old Richmond.* Richmond, 1941. Valentine Museum.

Scott, Mary Wingfield. *Old Richmond Neighborhoods.* Richmond, 1950. Published by the author.

Squires, W. H. T. *An Anthology of Virginia and Virginians.* A Volume of Manuscripts Presented to the State Library of Virginia.

Squires, W. H. T. *The Days of Yester-Year in Colony and Commonwealth.* Portsmouth, Virginia, 1928. Printcraft Press, Inc.

Squires, W. H. T. *Through Centuries Three.* A Short History of the People of Virginia. Portsmouth, Virginia, 1929. Printcraft Press, Inc.

Stanard, Mary Newton. *Colonial Virginia, Its People and Customs.* Philadelphia and London, 1917. J. B. Lippincott Company.

Stanard, Mary Newton. *The Story of Virginia's First Century.* Philadelphia and London, 1928. J. B. Lippincott Company.

Stanard, William G. and Stanard, Mary Newton. *The Colonial Virginia Register.* Albany, 1902. Joel Munsell's Sons, Publishers.

Stubbs, Dr. and Mrs. William Carter. *Descendants of Mordecai Cook of Mordecai's Mount, Gloucester County, Virginia 1650, and Thomas Booth of Ware Neck, Gloucester County, Virginia, 1685.* New Orleans, 1923. Published by Dr. and Mrs. William Carter Stubbs.

Stubbs, Dr. and Mrs. William Carter. *A History of Two Virginia Families, Transplanted from County Kent, England.* New Orleans, 1918. Published by Dr. and Mrs. Stubbs.

Tate, Leland B. *The Virginia Guide, The Land of the Life Worth Living.* A Manual of Information About Virginia. Lebanon, Virginia, 1929. Leland B. Tate.

Tuthill, William B. *Interiors and Interior Details.* New York, 1882. William T. Comstock, Architectural Publisher.

Verrill, A. Hyatt. *Romantic and Historic Virginia.* New York, 1935. Dodd Mead & Company.

Virginia Highway Historical Markers. Strasburg, Virginia, 1930. Shenandoah Publishing House, Inc.

Wallis, Frank E. *How to Know Architecture.* New York, 1910; 1914. Harper & Brothers, Publishers.

Waterman, Thomas Tileston and Barrows, John A. *Domestic Colonial Architecture of Tidewater Virginia.* New York—London, 1932. Charles Scribners Sons.

174

Waterman, Thomas Tileston. *The Dwellings of Colonial America.* Chapel Hill, 1950. The University of North Carolina Press.

Waterman, Thomas Tileston. *The Mansions of Virginia, 1706-1776.* Chapel Hill, 1945. The University of North Carolina Press.

Waterman, Thomas Tileston. *Thomas Jefferson, His Early Works in Architecture.* August 1943 number of *Gazette des Beaux-Arts.*

Williams, Henry Lionel and Williams, Ottalie K. *Old American Houses and How to Restore Them.* Garden City, New York, 1946. Doubleday & Company, Inc.

Wilstach, Paul. *Tidewater Virginia.* Indianapolis, 1929. The Bobbs-Merrill Company.

PERIODICALS

Calendar of Virginia State Papers.
Henings Statues of Virginia.
Lower Norfolk County Virginia Antiquary.
Tyler's Historical and Genealogical Quarterly.
Virginia Historical Register.
Virginia Magazine of History and Biography.
William and Mary Quarterly Historical Magazine—First Series.
William and Mary Quarterly Historical Magazine—Second Series.

CURRENT PUBLICATIONS

Commonwealth Magazine.
Virginia and the Virginia County.

NEWSPAPERS

Baltimore Sun.
Gloucester—Mathews Gazette—Journal.
New York Times.
Richmond News Leader.
Richmond Times Dispatch.